LOOK UP

LOOK UP

Our Story with the Stars

SARAH CRUDDAS

ONE PLACE. MANY STORIES

HQ
An imprint of HarperCollins*Publishers* Ltd
1 London Bridge Street
London SE1 9GF
This edition 2020

1

First published in Great Britain by
HQ, an imprint of HarperCollins*Publishers* Ltd 2020

ISBN: 978-0-00-835827-3
ISBN: 978-0-00-835828-0

MIX
Paper from
responsible sources
FSC
www.fsc.org   FSC™ C007454

This book is produced from independently certified FSC™ paper
to ensure responsible forest management.

For more information visit: www.harpercollins.co.uk/green

Printed and bound by
CPI Group (UK) Ltd, Croydon, CR0 4YY

For Agatha Reeves, the brightest star in the sky.

Contents

FOREWORD

by Gemini 10 and Apollo 11 astronaut
Michael Collins

n 1969, when I went to the Moon as part of the crew of Apollo 11, it was a dream come true. I had somehow lucked into being one third of the team that was going to do this wonderful thing. I had stumbled in at the right time, at the cusp between the old and the new.

We crew felt the weight of the world on our shoulders. We knew that everybody – friend or foe – would be looking at us. We wanted to do the best we possibly could. I wasn't scared, but I was worried. How could you fail to be, when you are undertaking something so extraordinary?

I always think of a flight to the Moon as being a long and fragile daisy chain of events. No matter how well things were going, I couldn't just relax and pat myself on the back. The flight was a question of being under constant tension, worried about what's coming next, and asking ourselves, what do I have to do now to keep this daisy chain intact? There were so many people involved in this mission, so many people counting on us and working for that same goal.

As I reflect on the work of a new generation of space technology, and the story that *Look Up* tells us, I feel the sense of that daisy chain still. It's our responsibility to keep that mission – that daisy chain – intact and moving forward; inspiring the next generation of adventurers.

As we prepared for Apollo 11, we spent a lot of time in simulators to be as ready as we could be for what we'd encounter. These simulators were at the heart and soul of our training. They were very powerful instruments and we couldn't have made it to the moon without them. But their one failing? They couldn't duplicate the view that we saw out of the window. To see the Moon up close is indescribable. It filled our window with its gigantic presence. Its belly bulging out towards us, bigger than you thought possible. Sunlight cascaded around its rim. The dark was somehow darker. The light was lighter. It was a magnificent spectacle. One few of us have had the honor to see.

If our story with the stars has taught us anything, it's that humankind has an innate desire to be outward bound, to continue traveling. People don't want to live in a box. They want to look up into the sky. They want to see things that they do not understand, to come to know them better, perhaps even physically go there and examine them. To see, to smell, to touch, to feel. We are wanderers. And eventually humans are going to leave and go places and live there. When I look up to the sky, I see all these miraculous, marvelous things. All I can think is we ought to lift the lid of that box and get going. On the occasions when I look at the Moon, I think, been there, done that! I regard the Moon, not so much as a destination, but as a direction for humanity's migration.

It's Mars that excites me the most, now. It was my favorite as a child, and still is today. When I came back from the Moon, I joked that NASA sent me to the wrong planet. Mars is the one we should have our eye on. Though it is inhospitable, it is the closest thing in our solar system that we have to a sister planet and going there would be a fascinating new frontier.

After the flight of Apollo 11, I remember so vividly the around the world trip that the three of us – Neil, Buzz and myself – took. We were surprised that everywhere we went, every city we visited, we were greeted not with 'oh well you Americans finally did it'. But we were greeted with we did it. We humanity. We human beings. I think we have to build on that spirit as we continue to explore.

Because if there is one thing more extraordinary even than seeing the Moon, it is seeing the Earth. As Apollo 8 astronaut Bill Anders pointed out, when you are up there, if you put your thumbnail in front of Earth, you could totally obscure it. But I found every time I removed my thumb, the Earth popped back into my view. It wanted to be seen. It was the whole show. It was my home, everything I knew. The white clouds and blue of the ocean. Background totally black. I will remember that all my life. It leaves one to consider, well, is it really so pretty? Is it as quiet as it looks? Is it really so pristine? As I looked at it, the word 'fragile' came up out of the murk somehow. I thought, it's a fragile little thing, isn't it?

And I don't think we are treating its fragility properly. Technology has brought us great benefits, but it has also come at a cost. We are using the Earth's resources at a rate unseen before. It seems that nearly every advance in our civilization has had some undesirable side effects, and it's up to the next generation of engineers, explorers, and thinkers, to forge a path that will help our planet, so that it can truly become the beautiful, tranquil gem it seems to be when viewed from the Moon.

During Apollo, the words of JFK helped us so much in our preparation for the first lunar landing. We had these succinct, wonderful instructions. And I'd like to transfer the spirit of President Kennedy's words from where we are today, to where we might go. The simplicity of his mandate of 'landing a man on the moon and returning him safely to the Earth' motivated those of us working to get to that goal. Future spaceflight can be limitless; using Kennedy's model, the *What*, *When*, and *How* will be determined by new generations. Whether that's a flight to Mars to take our next steps to the frontier, or to meet that challenge of climate change and our planet's finite resources head on, more people should be privileged to fly in space and get the chance to see the fragile earth as it appears from afar. I am happy to see the younger generation's excitement at continuing the legacy of outward bound. Sarah Cruddas is a gifted writer and *Look Up* is an inspired book. I am hopeful that we will never stop looking up.

Michael Collins, Gemini 10 and Apollo 11 astronaut, July 2020

INTRODUCTION

'I am tormented by an everlasting itch for things remote.'

Herman Melville

have never been to space. And it is most likely that neither have you. In fact, of the more than 100 billion humans that are estimated to have ever existed, fewer than 600 have made the journey away from our planet. Of those 600, only 24 have ventured as far as the Moon, with just 12 walking on its surface.

Before the middle of the twentieth century, the entire history of our species played out on a world that for so long was grand and full of mystery to us, but on a cosmic scale is frighteningly small – our home and everything we hold dear is but a speck in the vastness of the unknown. That is not to say that we are insignificant *per se*, merely that we are a mindbogglingly tiny part of something that we are yet to fully understand.

However, all of us alive today are living in a time when going to space is no longer a fantasy. In fact, it is something that has been proven to be possible; something that we perhaps even take for granted; and something that is rapidly developing and becoming an increasingly important part of our lives – often without us realising. We are part of a small but ever-growing fraction of our species that exists in a time when we are able to step outside our

Earthly home and begin to explore the unknowns of the universe.

The exploration of space is the most significant thing we will ever do collectively as a species. That might sound like a bold statement to make, but in setting foot into the grandeur of the universe, we are beginning to explore what it is that our planet is a part of. In doing so, we are pursuing answers to profound questions; ones that have been pondered by great minds throughout human existence.

Why do we exist? Where do we come from? Where are we heading? Are we alone? It is in our DNA to seek these answers. The same curiosity that has driven us to explore our Earth is now taking us to space. But in many ways, space exploration is as much about philosophy and a search for meaning as it is science. It is only by continuing to explore our surroundings that we can continue to find out more about ourselves.

Of course, sending humans and machines into space has brought many practical benefits, as well as literally changing our point of view of Earth. In space, we can conduct science experiments to help us better understand everything from the smallest cells in our body to the entire ecosystem of our planet. And it has shown us just how fragile our home really is. Astronauts can look back at Earth and see the thin blue line of our atmosphere; all that protects us and keeps us safe, we now know is overwhelmingly fragile.

It is one thing to say this, it is another thing to experience this first-hand, and to see Earth from space – a fragile marble hanging in the void, a long way from anything else. Seeing our home from this new vantage point has enabled us to gain knowledge about changes to our climate that are taking place and the inevitable problems we face should we not take action to limit them.

Most of all, the reason why space exploration is so significant is because it is our future. We cannot and should not remain still on our planet when we have the capabilities to leave it and see what is out there beyond the 'horizon'. It is that innate curiosity and yearning to push the boundaries of what is possible that has given us the world of today. And it is by continuing to explore our universe that we can give a future to generations to come – a future that perhaps we cannot quite imagine, just as previous generations could not have imagined the world we live in today. We owe it to them to keep moving. There is more to this universe than our Earthly home. In many ways, our survival as the human race is intrinsically linked to our curiosity and our ability to keep exploring.

But with all that is wrong in the world today, why should we focus our resources on space? Are there not more pressing needs here on Earth? There are so many problems facing us – from climate change, to political corruption, social injustice and the fact that the richest eight people on the planet have more wealth than the poorest three and a half billion. But the argument made by some that we shouldn't go to space and should instead look to the issues on Earth is misguided. I want to show you how so much of what we do in space is really about Earth, and how science conducted in space really does benefit every single person on the planet. Space is for everyone.

*

I have always been fascinated by space. One of my first memories is of looking up at the Moon and the night sky, using a pair of children's binoculars to stare at the lunar surface. I didn't know anyone who was a scientist, or an astronomer, but for as long as I can remember, space has been my passion.

When I was around eight years old, we learnt about the planets at school. I can vividly remember finding out about Venus and how it had this choking thick atmosphere. I was in awe of the different places that existed within our solar system – these worlds that were so strange and alien compared with our Earth. I consumed books, magazines and television documentaries about space, often ones far too advanced for my age. I had an insatiable appetite for learning more about this universe that we are a part of.

I spent my paper-round money on Glowstars that I arranged into the shapes of the constellations on my bedroom ceiling and I put up maps of the Moon's surface on my wall. I had a telescope and binoculars which I would use to explore the lunar surface, imagining what it must have been like for the astronauts who went there. I spent hours thinking about the possibility of one day going to space myself – what it would be like to ride a rocket, to float free in the microgravity environment, perhaps even to walk on the surface of Mars. Looking up filled me with wonder and gave me purpose.

My childhood was spent living on the outskirts of Hull. We had little money, but the stories I read about astronauts showed me that so much was possible through hard work and determination. My love of space became my driving force to work hard at my studies. I would constantly dream about the possibilities to come in the future – seeing humans travelling further away from Earth and setting foot on Mars.

As a teenager, I worked in a factory packing fruit so that I could pay to attend a space summer school in the UK and self-fund a GCSE in astronomy, which I taught myself at home. I just wanted to learn as much as possible. The more I learnt, the more questions I was left with. Everything fascinated me – from the origins of the universe to the wonders of the planets in our solar system.

In the year 2000, I entered a competition called the Young Scientist Award; the prize was a week at NASA's International Space Camp in Huntsville, Alabama. I can still remember the feeling of the knot in my stomach as I stepped out on stage to give my science presentation to an audience of hundreds of children and adults. My talk – which teenage me had smugly titled 'Where do babies come from?' – was the story of how you and I and everything we know of all come from stardust. The very atoms in your body were once part of a star. We are all part of the universe.

You can never underestimate the impact that giving an opportunity to a child can have on their future. I won the competition and travelled to NASA's Space Camp, a place that had previously seemed as far removed from the reality of my childhood as the Moon. It was an opportunity that taught me more about the value of hard work – that if you work hard, it doesn't matter where you come from, you can succeed. I would later go on to study Physics with Astrophysics at university, with ambitions of doing a PhD.

But somewhere along the line I got sidetracked. Instead of starting a PhD, after university I found myself training to become a journalist. My love of exploring the stars now sat alongside my newfound love of travel. As a student I had roamed around South America and it had opened my eyes to just how much inequality existed. I now wanted to show people the world, what I had seen. I wanted to tell stories. However, as any young person with big plans knows, you've got to start somewhere, and after stints as a freelance radio reporter, my first job was working for the BBC as a weather presenter for regional news.

But my passion for space stayed with me and so, alongside my day job, I decided to try to cover stories about space exploration in my free time. I interviewed astronauts and reported on the latest events, from meteor showers to missions to the planet Jupiter. Often I would get up at 3.30am to work an early presenting shift, then travel in the afternoon to interview someone. For a long time, it was only the overnight radio shows that would take my pieces about space, so I would find myself doing a pre-recorded broadcast at 10pm, before getting up in the early hours for my main job.

In July 2011, the Space Shuttle was scheduled to launch for the final time. I had never seen a rocket launch, but I knew I had to be there. I took three weeks' leave from the BBC and bought a flight to Florida. There wasn't really the need for an extra reporter, and I had no commissions, but I reasoned if I 'just happened to be there' they might use me. It was a gamble that paid off: not only did I witness the launch, but thirteen days later I found myself sat with my broadcast kit talking live on the radio as Space Shuttle *Atlantis* touched down in front of me – a defining moment for human spaceflight, the end of the shuttle programme.

Those three weeks in Florida changed me. I lived in a house on Cocoa Beach (not far from the Kennedy Space Center) with strangers who would become friends. I met scientists and experts within the industry. My days were spent at NASA and my nights in bars that were once frequented by America's first astronauts. The 'welcome home' banner for *Atlantis* that hangs at the Kennedy Space Center and that is covered in autographs includes my name. I felt like I was no longer an observer or a fan of the space industry, but that I was a part of it. And I learnt that if you really want something, you have to go after it. Life is not a dress rehearsal.

I ended up leaving my weather presenting job in 2012 to follow my dreams. I wanted to be part of the space industry, to tell stories about space exploration and show people the possibilities of our future. I wanted to use tales of those pioneers who helped us reach beyond Earth to show why space matters, and to inspire as many people as possible in their own lives. Through social media I saw how much enthusiasm there is for space – even though, at the time, the media appetite for it had waned.

The end of the Space Shuttle programme brought redundancies for many who had worked on it. NASA astronauts were no longer launching from American soil, and for a time, there was an uncertainty about what would happen next. The area around the Kennedy Space Center in Florida, once so busy and energised, felt eerily quiet. But in this lull, things started to change, and the commercial space industry, backed by private companies and entrepreneurs, started to grow. It was this new approach to space exploration that really captured my imagination.

Today, my job is a mix of working within the commercial space industry and with the public on television and radio, and by giving talks around the world. I have worked with and shared stages with astronauts, famous entrepreneurs, business leaders and politicians, travelling the globe and sharing my passion for space and how we can shape our future away from Earth. I have chased rocket launches and hosted TV shows on both sides of the Atlantic. My love of travel now forms part of my work, too.

My career has seen successes and moments that my younger self could have only dreamed of, but also many failures. It is one thing that my love of space and, particularly, my knowledge of the story of space exploration taught me as a child: you will probably fail, but you have to keep going. You won't get everything right, and you can't control all that happens to you, but it is how you deal with failing that matters most.

Today, NASA – which I so nervously walked into as a teenager – is a place I know well. I have been lucky enough to watch countless sunsets from Cocoa Beach in Florida, and this area around the Kennedy Space Center is one of my favourite places in the world. Not only is it full of history that dates back to when we first stepped away from Earth, but it is also a place full of possibility, and history yet to be written. Happily, it is also now once again thriving with many new space companies, as space slowly becomes more accessible to us all.

When people ask me why I care so much, my answer is always the same: why would you *not* be interested in space? It is the story of who we are. There is so much to explore and discover. Why wouldn't you want to be a part of finding out what is out there?

Wherever I go and whatever I do, I always remember to look up at the stars – be that insisting on taking the window seat on a night flight so I can glimpse the Moon, or simply stepping outside of wherever I happen to be staying in a far-flung corner of the world. Those moments spent looking up continue to inspire me and to fuel my passion as to why exploring space matters so much. A human lifetime is so terrifyingly short, but I hope that I can use my time to play a small part in advancing humanity into space. You never know who you might end up inspiring. My contribution to our species' future is to play a tiny part in the space industry – this great adventure into the universe that is only just beginning.

*

A lot of the time, space exploration can seem far removed from our day-to-day lives. But the reality is that it is far closer than you perhaps realise. According to NASA, space begins at just 50 miles up – though there is some dispute about this, with other international organisations saying space begins at just over 60 miles. The discrepancy is because the Earth's atmosphere does not end abruptly, instead slowly thinning. There is no sign announcing, 'You are now leaving Earth'.

The distance from where you are now 'up' to the International Space Station – our 'off-world' outpost and home to normally six astronauts at any one time – is less than the distance between Newcastle and London: roughly 250 miles. Anyone born after November 2000 has never known a time when humans haven't been living and working in space, as the International Space Station has been permanently crewed by a rotation of astronauts since then.

A journey from launch to orbit, though, is shorter than to the docking stations at the ISS, taking just eight and a half minutes. So not only is space far closer that you might realise, but today it doesn't even take very long to get there. Yet making this journey 'up' just a matter of miles is something that would take humankind until the last century to be able to achieve.

Since 1957 – when Sputnik became the first human-made object to travel to space – we have been incrementally pushing the limits of how far we can go and what we can do beyond Earth. Our knowledge and understanding of space – along with our place within it – has increased exponentially over these past six decades. And even though the furthest that humans have travelled is to the Moon, we have sent robotic craft out beyond that to begin to explore the other worlds with whom we share our cosmic address.

Spacecraft have studied our Sun, trying to make sense of the complex relationship we have with the star that gives us life. They have orbited and mapped out Mercury and landed on Venus, sending back images and scientific details before being crushed and melted under the intense heat and pressure. On Mars, we have sent rovers to roam the surface. Operated from Earth, they conduct experiments in search of signs of past and present life and send back images of the arid, rocky Martian landscape with its milky pink sky, where hopefully one day humans will walk. And in other explorations we have orbited the gas giants Jupiter and Saturn and flown by the ice giants Uranus and Neptune – frigidly cold worlds where scientists suspect diamonds may rain from the clouds.

At the far reaches of the solar system we have visited

Pluto. When the New Horizons mission launched from Earth in 2006, Pluto was still known as the 'ninth planet'. By the time the spacecraft arrived, in 2015 – giving us our first ever view of this distant, frozen world where volcanos may spew ice – Pluto had been reclassified as a dwarf planet. It is now known to be the first of many dwarf planets that exist in our solar system, worlds that are essentially round like a planet, but not massive enough to dominate their orbital paths. While we think we know much about the universe around us, we actually know so little – our understanding is constantly evolving.

Step by step, we are slowly peering out into our cosmic surroundings. We have gained a view of our solar system that even a matter of a century ago would have seemed impossible. We have studied asteroids and chased and landed on a comet. Each robotic space mission brings about new surprises as we explore further than ever before, watching as the mysteries of space begin to unravel before us.

We have also begun to understand the inconceivable enormity of the universe, where our own Sun is just one of many billions of stars in our galaxy, the Milky Way. And our Milky Way galaxy is one of many billions of galaxies that exist in the universe. There are trillions of stars and probably many more planets. Thanks to advances in our understanding of space – helped by telescopes in orbit – we now have a high degree of confidence that for pretty much every star you can see in the night sky, there is at least one planet orbiting around it. Our solar system is one of many.

Just think about that next time you look up. Think about how weird and wonderful the planets in our own solar system are, then, looking at those stars in the night sky, just imagine – if you can – what could possibly be out there, orbiting those many, many other suns. So far, we have discovered rocky worlds orbiting stars at just the right distance to have the conditions needed for liquid water. There are planets so close to their sun that they zip around it in a matter of days, and we have even discovered a world which scientists believe is made largely of diamond. Whenever I write about other planets, it often seems like science fiction to talk of how alien these worlds are compared with our own. The reality of what we keep discovering is often stranger than any fiction.

At the moment, though, the only place in this impossibly vast universe full of trillions of stars and planets where we know for sure life exists is here, on planet Earth. Proving there is life elsewhere in the solar system has so far evaded our greatest technology and our brightest minds. The universe could be teaming with life; there could even be life on a simple scale within our own solar system. Or we could be totally alone, the sole inhabitants of an impossible, unforgiving universe – our existence and ability to question it down to pure chance. Looking at the numbers, that is highly unlikely, but not impossible. We just don't know yet. But I for one hope that we are not all alone.

We have studied the formation of planets and conducted research that is helping us to begin to piece together how our own existence came to be. We have photographed the birth of stars and distant galaxies and looked back billions of years into the universe, helped by powerful space-based telescopes, free from the disturbance of our Earth's atmosphere.

However, compared with how big the universe is (some 93 billion light years in diameter, according to current thinking), we have barely begun to scratch the surface of what is out there. For each new discovery, we are often left with more questions than answers. But all of that possibility and all of those things that we can't yet explain are what make going to space so exciting; the unknowns, and all the unimaginable things to come. It allows us to dream and wonder what else is out there, what we are a part of. Best of all, this ability to wonder about space is accessible to every single one of us – all you have to do is look up.

Of course, this ability to look up won't by itself solve many of the immediate or pressing problems that we now face, but it does bring about a sense of belonging and wonder, which I think we all so desperately need now, more than ever. When we look up at the night sky, it is like we are peering out of a window of our Earthly home and out into the universe. We are a part of something greater, though we can't quite fully comprehend what it is. No matter what we face on Earth, knowing that we are all in this together offers a notion of comfort. What divides us on Earth – borders, class, race – means nothing in the universe. We all call the same planet home. The borders we use to divide us on Earth are meaningless when we leave.

*

The year 2019 was an incredible one for space exploration. All over the world, people celebrated the fiftieth anniversary of when humans first landed on the Moon, but they also looked to the possibilities that lie before us over the next 50 years. Though we haven't been back to the Moon since December 1972 – when Apollo 17 became the last lunar landing – the fiftieth anniversary of the first landing came at a time when there was a renewed drive to keep exploring space. And the greatest way to honour those first pioneers of space was to look to the future.

On 20 July 2019, I sat on the National Mall in Washington, DC, not far from the Washington Monument, on a humid summer evening as a sea of people counted down to the exact moment when humans first set foot on the Moon. As video screens played out that historic footage of Neil Armstrong walking down the ladder of the Lunar Module, the crowd around me cheered. At that moment I felt more than ever that space mattered and I was so proud to play my small part in the industry.

Space exploration was getting the public attention it deserves and many – not just those within the niche bubble of the industry – were talking enthusiastically about what was next; people from all walks of life were beginning to get excited about continuing to explore space. At the same time, government agencies such as NASA, along with the many new private companies, were talking of bold plans for our space future, including returning humans to the Moon under the Artemis Program. It felt like a new era in space was opening up.

I started writing this book in that summer of 2019, not just because I wanted to inspire as many people as possible about why space matters, but also to try to explain the importance of this new era in space exploration that we are entering. I wanted to share not only the passion that has defined my entire life, but also the hope and possibility that space gives us. To encourage all of us to step away from our smartphones and technology, and look up with a knowledge of why we explore space, how it has shaped our lives and how it will transform those of generations to come. No matter where you are from, who you are, or what you do, space is for all of us – and we all use space technology far more than you probably think.

*

There are so many amazing stories to tell of the people who made our journey into space possible. I have chosen the ones that inspire me – some well known, others less so. Of course, no book about space exploration would be complete without the story of how we first took to the stars. The space race took place in the shadow of the Cold War, and in that sense it was fuelled by darkness and fear, and yet it ultimately showed us what could be achieved when we united towards a huge, audacious goal.

Today, what many call the Apollo Generation – those who made the Apollo Moon landings possible – are almost gone. We have lost nearly all of those who enabled us to go to the Moon. But their work laid the foundations for everything we do in space. That is why it is important that their story continues to be told. Within the space industry, the phrase 'standing on the shoulders of giants' is often used to refer to the work we have done since we first left Earth. Nothing we do in space would be possible without those early pioneers.

But behind every endeavour in space exploration are tales of ordinary people who have done extraordinary things. It is these tales that helped to inspire my lifelong love of space. Leaving Earth is not just about science or wonder, but it is also a very human story – one of dedication, determination and sacrifice. In the face of great losses and personal risk, people still choose to travel to space, drawn to it as if to a higher calling.

And, despite the incredible achievements of the Apollo generation, the world we live in today is not what we expected it to be back in the 1960s. But the reality is that we are living in a space age of a different kind. It might not look how we imagined, but we use space technology every single day. In fact, the many satellites in orbit which look back at Earth have helped transform all of our lives.

In many ways, we are now entering an entrepreneurial space age, which is helping to shape our future. Today, going to space is no longer just about governments, but also private companies and individuals. These investors are changing how we get to space and what we can achieve once we are there. Humans will return to the Moon, they will go onwards to Mars and beyond, and they will continue to use space to benefit us all, thanks in part to these entrepreneurs. Though some of their visions and ambitions might seem bold, it is the ability of these people to go against the status quo and their willingness to embrace failure that are helping us to go further than ever before.

If you look back to the beginning of the last century and see just how much we have achieved in little more than one human lifetime, you can begin to realise how far we will go in this century. My hope is that one day our knowledge of science and technology will have advanced to the point where we can grasp more comprehensively our place within the universe and explore all the untold possibilities that lie before us. Though those stars you can see when you look up are too far for us to reach now, perhaps one day we will find a way.

And finally, of all the things we are doing and have done in space, the greatest achievement is the new perspective we have gained. It is a shift in perspective so powerful that it has reduced to tears some who have experienced it for themselves and given all a newfound love of our planet. Images of our world, showing us as a fragile blue marble with swirls of white clouds set against an ink-black backdrop, seemingly floating in nothingness, are perhaps more poignant and profound today than ever before. In space we are united; we all call the same world home. And in order to continue to explore and to go further, we will need to work together. Exploring beyond Earth is bigger than any one nation or individual.

All of us alive today are part of the privileged few, those who live in a time when humans are no longer confined to one planet, but have the ability to step beyond and begin to discover what is out there. We are all part of the Space Age and the pursuit of knowledge beyond our planet will benefit all of us.

*

Space exploration teaches us that we are all interconnected, and that when we come together we are capable of great things – a lesson that speaks volumes for us right now. It also shows us the value of science, and that scientific research into every aspect of our being is imperative for our ability to survive the great challenges that we face as a species. But perhaps most importantly, space gives us hope. It gives us the ability to dream, to wonder and to understand that we are all in this together. The possibilities to come from the unknowns of the universe and the sense of wonder gained from looking up at the stars fill me with optimism.

I am finishing writing this book in the spring of 2020, in lockdown. A time when the world has been changed by a global pandemic, but the value of science has never been so abundantly clear. Recently, I have found myself looking up at the stars more than ever. Doing so is a reminder of how tiny we are compared with the vastness of what is out there. It is a notion that has helped me to deal with the various hurdles and problems I have faced in my own life, and it continues to do so in the challenging moments of our current existence. There is still beauty in all of this chaos.

So, on that note, I want to finish with a story about two spacecraft. You may have heard of Voyager 1 and Voyager 2, the twin robotic spacecraft that launched 16 days apart from each other in 1977. Their mission was a journey across our solar system, initially to explore the gas giants Jupiter and Saturn, studying Saturn's rings and learning about some of the moons of the two planets. They were designed to last for five years – long enough so they could complete their mission.

The initial stages of their journey saw the spacecraft study Jupiter's atmosphere, uncovering many hurricane-like storms and photographing up close the Great Red Spot – a storm almost three times larger than our Earth that has raged on the planet for centuries. They discovered active volcanoes on Jupiter's moon, Io, and indications of a liquid ocean beneath the icy surface of another moon, Europa. At Saturn, they sent back close-up images of the planet's rings and found frozen moons shaped by ice volcanoes.

At this point, NASA extended the missions of the two little Voyagers, to keep on exploring. Their five-year lifetimes were stretched out to twelve years and remote programming from Earth allowed the craft to be updated with more modern capabilities. Voyager 1 studied the deep smoggy atmosphere of Saturn's moon, Titan – the only moon in our solar system that has its own atmosphere, whilst Voyager 2 travelled to the planets Uranus and Neptune. At Uranus it discovered ten new moons orbiting the planet. And at Neptune it discovered a dark spot where winds rage at over one thousand miles per hour and geysers erupt from the poles of the planet's largest moon, Triton. To date, Voyager 2 is the only spacecraft to ever visit these two giant icy balls of gas billions of miles away from us.

With their respective missions complete, Voyager 1 and Voyager 2 continued travelling further away from Earth and to the far reaches of our solar system. Even though they were well beyond their expected lifetimes they were still able to communicate via radio signal to scientists back on Earth.

On Valentine's Day 1990 – at the insistence of the famed cosmologist Carl Sagan – Voyager 1 turned its camera around and pointed it back at Earth. From a distance of four billion miles away, the spacecraft took a photograph. The image, even after being magnified, shows a small pale speck in a corner. The speck is so tiny that if nobody pointed it out, you would probably not notice it. But that tiny speck is all of us. And it is where Sagan's name for our Earth, 'The Pale Blue Dot', came from.

That day, Voyager 1 collected many more photographs

that showed six of the other planets in our solar system – Venus, Mars, Jupiter, Saturn, Uranus and Neptune. All vast unexplored worlds but, from the edge of our solar system, they too looked like tiny bright specks. Stitched together as a mosaic, this became our 'family portrait'. It will most likely take many human lifetimes to even begin to complete our exploration of what lies within this mosaic.

In 2012, almost 35 years since its launch, Voyager 1 left the solar system and became the first human-made object to reach what is known as interstellar space – the region of space that is beyond the influence and protective bubble of our own Sun or any other star systems. Six years later, in 2018, Voyager 2 followed suit. To save power, the cameras on both spacecraft have been turned off and slowly their instruments will be shut down by scientists. At the moment, the twin craft can still communicate with Earth – a round trip to send and receive data takes more than a day. It is hoped that the spacecraft will be able to transmit signals back to Earth until 2036.

Heading in different directions, when transmissions finally stop, the two spacecrafts will each wander alone in the universe. In the year 40,272, Voyager 1 will pass 1.7 light years from the star Gliese 445. And around the same time Voyager 2 will pass by a small star called Ross 248. Both these stars can be seen here from Earth; they are objects in our night sky that humans have looked up at since our beginnings. Thousands of years from now, two pieces of humanity will have finally reached the stars.

Perhaps by this time, humans will have developed the technology to travel further than we can dream of. They may even catch up with the two Voyagers. But even if they don't, the spacecraft will still continue on their journeys. Passing by clouds of dust, blown out by dying stars into the vacuum of space.

On board each spacecraft is a twelve-inch disc, known as the Golden Record. These gold-plated phonograph records each contain 'murmurs of Earth' – the sounds of our planet and spoken greetings in 55 different languages. They also house electronic images of what life was like in the 1970s – sporting events, families with children, islands in the ocean, dancers and traffic jams in Thailand, as well as details of our anatomy, the structure of our DNA, a map of the planet and a photograph of Earth. Our first cosmic messages in a bottle; a time capsule of who we once were.

Also etched on one side of each record are details of where the two spacecraft have travelled from. Should an extra-terrestrial civilisation ever happen to come across one of the Voyagers, they will be able to decipher the precise location of Earth and how long the crafts have been travelling for. Although in the scale of the universe the chances are slim – the Voyagers are effectively needles in a vast cosmic haystack – there is a small possibility that someone or something might one day discover the first human-made objects to venture beyond our solar system.

In about five billion years' time, our Sun will swell and die. Earth and the solar system we are only just exploring will be no more. But it is likely that the Voyager spacecraft will still exist – albeit without power. They will spend an eternity wandering through space. Two pieces of the universe that will forever be part of humankind.

In the timespan of one human lifetime, we will not have all the answers to what is out there. We may never have all the answers, but why wouldn't you want to at least try? To be part of the adventure. We have a choice: remain alone and isolated on this island in the universe that is Earth, or step out into the ocean of our cosmos. All the wonders of the stars above us await.

Prologue

DARING TO DREAM

'Curiosity is the essence of human existence.'

Gene Cernan

We are born explorers.

Human beings have always been driven by a desire to know what is over the next hill, on the other side of the river, or across the ocean. In the course of our history, our journeys of discovery may have been motivated by a desire to get rich, to expand our country's territory or to escape from something at home. But it's our innate curiosity and our ability to wonder what else is out there that prompted us to make the first steps into the jungle or cast off from the quayside.

Of course, our human curiosity has turned out very badly for some individuals, who took huge risks and paid the ultimate price. But it is this fundamental curiosity that has driven us forward as a species. We love to learn, we yearn to understand what is out there, and leaving the beaten track has taught us a lot of valuable lessons. Our world of today is owed to those who pushed the limits of what is possible; who had a restless urge to know what was over that next hill. Each generation has built on the knowledge gained as a result of the extraordinary risks taken by those who came before them – be that exploring the land around us, sailing the great oceans or taming the skies.

Our quest to discover Earth has gone hand in hand with our fascination with the stars and the universe above us. For nearly as long as there have been people, we have been captivated by space. Cave paintings found at various sites in Europe – some possibly dating back as far as 40,000 years – not only depict hunting scenes and people, but also patterns of the stars in the sky. These primitive star charts were most likely used as a form of time-keeping and demonstrate that our prehistoric ancestors were – like us – looking up.

As civilisations developed, so too did our knowledge and understanding of the stars, and we started to more carefully map and measure what we saw. From Egypt to Babylon, India to China, Greece to Rome and Mesoamerica, there is evidence of humans studying the night sky and using what they could see to better understand life on Earth. Observing the movement of the Sun across the sky and the phases of the Moon led us to develop calendars and learn to tell the time. In Ancient Egypt, for example, the knowledge was used to better plan when to plant and harvest crops, which in turn helped to advance agriculture.

The word 'planet' owes its origins to the Ancient Greeks who, like many other civilisations, noticed five star-like objects that, over time, slowly moved through the constellations. Greek astronomers called these points of light *asteres planetai*, or 'wandering stars'; today we know they were looking not at stars but at the planets Mercury, Venus, Mars, Jupiter and Saturn.

But, lacking in knowledge about the solar system and

our place within it, many at the time thought the planets were deities. We owe the names we use for them today in English (and other Latin-based languages) to the Romans, who named them in honour of their gods. The vastness of the night sky and the movement of the celestial bodies were so beyond our comprehension for most of human history that we told ourselves stories of gods and demons to explain them. In Hinduism, eclipses were explained by the demon Rahu briefly getting hold of the Sun or Moon. In Norse mythology, the Sun and Moon are pursued by two wolves, Hati and Skoll, who sometimes briefly catch up with them. And in Ancient China, it was believed that during an eclipse the Sun was eaten by a dragon, and it was necessary to bang on drums to frighten it away – a superstition that persisted even after Chinese astronomers learnt to predict when an eclipse would happen.

Our oldest science – astronomy – also aided our exploration of Earth. Navigation relied on it. Before the compass (invented in China in the eleventh century), the stars guided explorers as they sought to understand the world around them and expand their civilisations. For a long time, the geography of our planet – something we take for granted today – was continually evolving. For many centuries, while Europe languished in the Dark Ages, Chinese and Islamic thinkers and explorers led the way in understanding the world. But by the fifteenth century, some European nations – spurred on by the prospect of expanding their trading routes – were poised to catch up, with huge consequences for the world we know today.

In 1519, Ferdinand Magellan set sail from Seville with a fleet of five ships and a crew of 270 men. Their voyage was being bankrolled by the King of Spain and the intention was to find an alternative passage to the Spice Islands – now the Moluccas, in modern-day Indonesia – by heading west around the globe instead of taking the established easterly route. Few educated people at this time thought the world was flat, but some of Magellan's contemporaries still suspected the voyage wasn't even possible. The problem, though, was the size of the Earth, not its shape.

Polynesian people had explored the Pacific, settling on the islands they discovered – from Hawaii to Easter Island – starting perhaps as far back as 3,000 BCE. However, at the beginning of the sixteenth century, the most Europeans knew about what we now call the Pacific Ocean was that there was some sort of 'south sea' on the other side of the Americas. They had absolutely no idea of the scale of the ocean Magellan was planning to cross, nor how to find a sea passage into it. Yet despite the dangers, the arduous conditions they would experience on board, and the fear of sea monsters and storms, sailors joined Magellan's crew. They were motivated by the riches they could gain if they were successful – the spice trade was incredibly lucrative at the time. But there were still less dangerous ways to make money. Magellan and crew were daring to dream an impossible dream. It had only been 20 years since Vasco da Gama had become the first European to travel around the Cape of Good Hope and make it to India.

Of the five ships that set sail, only one made it back to Spain. Many – Magellan included – died during the attempt. While Magellan succeeded in finding and crossing through a strait at the foot of South America – which would go on to be named after him – he had to face a mutiny from his crew beforehand, and only regained control after beheading and marooning some of the mutineers. Those that survived the scurvy and starvation that ensued on their 98-day crossing of an expanse of water far bigger than anyone had imagined became the first Europeans to sail the Pacific Ocean.

Magellan himself died in the Philippines after picking a fight with a local king, but those 18 expedition members who survived the three-year voyage to return to Seville became the first humans to ever circumnavigate the globe. They had undertaken a voyage nobody else had. Something which to so many had seemed impossible, was now possible.

This period in European history is known as the Age of Exploration. It radically reshaped the world as we then knew it, and wreaked devastation on countless indigenous peoples. The Portuguese prince often called Henry the Navigator is credited with making a big contribution to exploration as he commissioned many expeditions at a time when lots of sailors were afraid of setting out into the Atlantic Ocean, tasking them with recording as much information as they could about the coastlines they visited. However, Henry was also responsible for starting the Atlantic slave trade. So when we celebrate humanity's drive to explore, at the same time it is also important to reflect on the horrendous mistakes we made.

The desire to discover new lands for their nations pushed shipbuilders, cartographers and astronomers to come up with better technology. A new type of ship, the caravel – capable of faster speeds and with manoeuvrable sails allowing it to tack into the wind – helped to make the voyages of Magellan and many others possible. Explorers also had to learn how to live on board ship for long periods of time, though how to prevent scurvy – the eventually deadly consequence of depriving the body of vitamin C – wasn't understood until the eighteenth century. Our desire to explore has continued to help push the limits of our understanding of the sciences of medicine and physiology.

At the same time as we were sending ships to further-away places, great minds were looking up and challenging the established ideas about the universe, often going against the thinking of religion. On his deathbed in 1543, the Polish astronomer Nicolaus Copernicus published his book *On the Revolutions of Celestial Spheres*. For more than a thousand years, we had believed the Earth was at the centre of the solar system; the Sun, the known planets and the stars all travelled around the Earth. But Copernicus's work challenged the idea upheld by the church. He stated that the Sun, not the Earth, was in fact at the centre of the solar system. His book was met with controversy, but it led the way to the Scientific Revolution and a new way of understanding our world. Among the great inventions of this period was the telescope, which opened up the wonders above us like never before.

Then, in 1768, the Royal Society and the British Admiralty sent James Cook to sail to Tahiti, where he and his crew aboard the *Endeavour* would observe the transit of Venus. This is when Venus appears to cross the Sun, as viewed from Earth. The transit of Venus occurs in pairs, eight years apart, every 120 years or so. Scientists at the Royal Society hoped that observing this phenomenon from the Pacific Ocean would expand their knowledge of the solar system. At the time, we understood that there were six planets, including Earth. Astronomers knew the relative spacing of these planets but what was a great mystery was the size of the solar system. It was hoped that by measuring Venus crossing our Sun from different locations on Earth, and noting the start and stop times, it would be possible to calculate how far away the planet is from Earth and therefore deduce an estimate of the size of the known solar system.

Using special telescopes, Cook and his onboard astronomer Charles Green observed the transit. But the intense sunlight filtering through Venus's atmosphere made the edge of the disc of the planet fuzzy, meaning it was difficult to get precise timings. The times recorded by Cook and Green differed by 42 seconds, and there were many variations in the other measurements recorded elsewhere in the world. It would take until the nineteenth century and the next pair of transits for astronomers to get the precise measurements needed – this time aided by photography.

Cook then continued with the second part of his mission and headed south, in search of 'Terra Australis Incognita'. Dutch, and possibly Portuguese, explorers had visited parts of Australia's coast already, but it wasn't known for sure whether this was the southern continent that many scientists believed must exist to 'balance' the landmass of the northern hemisphere.

After he first arrived in New Zealand and mapped it, Cook concluded that it was two islands and not what he was looking for. He finally sighted what he would name New South Wales on 19 April 1770 and 'claimed' it for Britain. The result of his discovery was that it was now possible to draw a reasonably accurate map of the world. Our picture of our home planet had changed completely since 1492, when Christopher Columbus had arrived in the Caribbean and believed it to be Asia.

Before the Age of Exploration began in the fifteenth century, the oceans had been the great frontier. But by embarking on these bold journeys and pushing the limits of where humans could go, we gained a better understanding of the Earth's geography. These impossible voyages also opened the door to future expeditions that would focus on scientific discovery rather than conquest and riches. In many ways, the voyage of the *Endeavour* was comparable to our space missions of today – Cook and his crew set sail both to conduct scientific research and to expand what we knew about our surroundings.

*

As we increased our knowledge of our planet and our understanding of science, our attention began to turn to the skies. People have always been fascinated by the idea of flying and the ability of birds to leave *terra firma* and rise high above us. The first real studies into the possibilities of flight were made by Leonardo da Vinci in the 1480s. Centuries ahead of his time, he produced over 100 drawings to illustrate his theories, and he famously drew a design for something that looks a lot like the modern helicopter. However, the ability to successfully rise above the ground and travel in the air had so far evaded us.

Then, on 19 September 1783, a crowd of dignitaries including King Louis XVI and Marie Antoinette gathered in Paris, France, to watch the flight of the Montgolfier balloon. I like to imagine that the atmosphere was comparable to the crowds watching the first crewed rocket launches on Florida's Space Coast almost two centuries later. The Montgolfier brothers behind the first hot air balloon were the Elon Musks of their day. They had made their money in paper manufacturing – a high-tech industry at the time – and were now pioneering a new type of technology.

The passengers for this flight were a duck, a sheep and a cockerel. No one had yet been up in the Montgolfiers' invention as they didn't know at the time if people could survive at altitude. The animals had been selected carefully; the thinking was that the sheep mimicked the physiology of a human, the duck was seen as unlikely to be harmed (as they already fly) and the cockerel was a control – cockerels are birds, but they do not fly. The animals survived their eight-minute journey, and humans would shortly follow them into the skies.

Two months later, Jean-François Pilâtre de Rozier and François Laurent le Vieux d'Arlandes sailed high above the rooftops of Paris – to the astonishment of its citizens – in the first crewed, untethered flight. Europe became gripped by balloonmania and its early pioneers were celebrities of the time.

Scientists, engineers and designers – and the people or organisations who bankroll their work – bring us great technological breakthroughs, enabling things to be done that have never been done before. But in order to achieve anything, you first have to come up with the idea. As Albert Einstein famously said, 'Imagination is more important than knowledge.' And for nearly as long as we have understood the Moon to be our satellite, and another world, rather than a deity or object in danger of being eaten by a wolf or dragon, we have imagined what it might be like to go there.

By the late nineteenth century, our understanding of science and technology had boomed as the Age of Enlightenment brought about a new understanding of the world around us. In turn, this knowledge helped inspire the imagination of artists and writers. Works of science fiction began to depict voyages to space. Jules Verne's eerily prophetic *From the Earth to the Moon* of 1865 and its sequel *Around the Moon,* told the tale of three

Americans launched from Florida bound on a voyage to the Moon, who later splashed down in the Pacific Ocean. Little more than 100 years later, three astronauts would do just that – launch from Florida bound on a mission to the Moon. Science fiction became science prediction.

One of the greatest ever writers of adventure stories, Jules Verne was born in 1828 in the French coastal city of Nantes. He grew up on stories of shipwrecks and nautical travels, and watched sailors at the docks close to where he lived arrive back from remote and far-flung places. The books he wrote as an adult were about impossible voyages and daring expeditions, but they were grounded in meticulously researched scientific fact and inspired by our real-life adventures on Earth. Verne's story about a voyage to the Moon would go on to inspire one of the first movies, Georges Méliès's *Le Voyage dans la Lune*. The 13-minute film captivated audiences in 1902, showing a crew of explorers shot from a cannon into the eye of the Moon.

Then, the following year, on 17 December 1903, on a windswept beach in Kitty Hawk, North Carolina, humans became capable of powered flight. Two bicycle builders, Orville and Wilbur Wright, successfully flew the aeroplane they had designed. The initial trip lasted just seconds, but it ignited the age of aviation. The skies became the new frontier.

Aviation's pioneers continually pushed the limits of where flight could take us. This new technology developed quickly and captured the imagination of the public. In

1927, Charles Lindbergh became the first person to travel solo across the Atlantic by aeroplane, flying from New York to Paris. His journey took 33.5 hours. A great ocean, which for so long could only be crossed by an arduous sea voyage, had been traversed in less than two days.

This new frontier of flight, of course, came with high risks. Many of the famed pilots of the era – among them Amelia Earhart, the first woman to fly solo across the Atlantic – lost their lives in the pursuit of extending our airborne capabilities. But in spite of the risks and the dangers, people continued in their quest to tame the sky. The spirit of adventure and yearning to fly called loudly to a new generation of explorers.

The demands of the Second World War brought yet more development in flight as aircraft became larger as well as capable of flying further and faster. Then in 1947 Chuck Yeager did something which had once been thought impossible – in a specially designed craft, the Bell X-1, he flew at over 800mph, faster than the speed of sound. Until this point it was unknown what would happen if someone in a plane attempted to cross what had been dubbed 'the sound barrier'.

As many remained captivated by the developments of aviation, other great minds looked very seriously at the feasibility of humans leaving Earth. Robert Goddard, Hermann Oberth, Konstantin Tsiolkovsky and Robert Esnault-Pelterie would become known as the 'Fathers of Rocketry'. Inspired by great works of science fiction, at the turn of the twentieth century they worked independently to develop the mathematics and techniques that would form the basics for us to eventually leave Earth by rocket. Voyages to space were no longer the stuff of science fiction, but instead within our grasp.

The stage was set for the stars.

On 4 May 1989, Magellan once again set out to explore the unknown. This time it was the *Magellan* spacecraft, launched by NASA to reach the orbit of Venus and map the planet's surface. It became one of NASA's most successful deep-space missions, just over 200 hundred years after those aboard James Cook's HMS *Endeavour* watched the planet cross the Sun from the deck of their ship. NASA has often named spacecraft for the great explorers who set out to learn more about our planet or their ships – the Space Shuttle *Endeavour* was named after James Cook's ship, and the name would later be used for the first SpaceX Crew Dragon capsule to be flown with astronauts onboard, while the Space Shuttle *Challenger* owed its name to the British Navy research vessel HMS *Challenger,* which explored the Atlantic and Pacific Oceans in the 1870s.

In many ways, space was our next natural step. Once we had sailed the great oceans, mapped the land and mastered the skies, it was inevitable that we would want to go further. So while our contemporary space scientists and engineers are working at the edge of what we currently know how to do, in some ways this is nothing new. We have always pushed at the boundaries of what we are capable of – figuring out how to achieve the impossible is how we move forward as a species. Our world of today, for better and worse, is owed to those who set sail in search of new horizons.

Today, the distance between the planets in our solar system is like the span of the oceans between the continents for those in the Age of Exploration. Just like our ancestors, we are setting sail into the unknown on voyages that will bring about new discoveries, knowledge and benefits that we cannot even imagine. History has taught us that, by building on the knowledge of previous generations, things which once seemed impossible eventually become possible.

Chapter One

THE SPACE RACE

'Far better it is to dare mighty things.'

President Theodore Roosevelt

n 1969, more than 40 years on from its invention, television had become a mainstay of nearly every American household. Although there were only three main networks and the majority of people still only had access to black and white TV, this new way of communicating was now firmly entrenched. Families would gather round to watch everything from the news to political debates, soap operas and cartoons.

The decade had been a tumultuous one for the American people, and both the triumphs and the horrors had been broadcast into homes across the country. They had watched, many with hope, as a youthful and charismatic John F. Kennedy was sworn in to office as the thirty-fifth president of the United States, promising peace and progress in the midst of the Cold War. Less than three years later he was dead. Scheduled programmes were interrupted to broadcast news of his assassination, the footage from Dallas showing a stunned Jackie Kennedy still wearing her suit covered in her husband's blood. Days later, viewers saw their young son, John Jr, saluting his father's flag-draped casket during the televised public funeral that was held on his third birthday.

For the first time, TV coverage of the Vietnam War

brought footage of combat into the home. And it showed the reality of the civil rights movement and Martin Luther King Jr's impassioned call for equality as he stood in front of the Lincoln Memorial in Washington, DC, and uttered the words 'I have a dream.' Then, in April 1968, he too was shot dead.

The television that families gathered around had become the stage on which the jeopardy of the decade – under the persistent threat of all-out nuclear war with the Soviet Union – was played out. And famed news anchors such as Walter Cronkite became part of the family as they delivered news of both promise and heartbreak. Cronkite was the godfather of broadcast journalism, his authority and consistent presence with the CBS Evening News making him to many 'the most trusted man in America'.

Thanks to advances in broadcasting, and for the first time communications satellites, stories from around the globe could be brought to living rooms faster. With the birth of the Space Age had come Telstar 1 in 1962, which meant live television could be transmitted between the US and Europe for the first time. Soon after, more communication satellites followed. While the act of going to space fascinated many, the ability to see live images from around the world thanks to satellites in space had a huge impact on the lives of many more. Space had started to show people the world.

On the afternoon of 20 July 1969, Americans were once again huddled around their television sets. 'In just 50 minutes from now, well within the hour, the Moon is due to have visitors from another planet,' began Cronkite, as he addressed the nation. As the minutes ticked down, coverage cut away to shots of people surrounding television screens across the country, from the arrivals lounges at airports to Disneyland in California. In the studio, alongside Cronkite sat Wally Schirra, one of the original Mercury Seven – America's first group of astronauts. As the minutes turned to seconds, the two men joined viewers in holding their breath. Apollo 11's Lunar Module was moments away from landing on the Moon.

Screens turned to a simulation of how the lunar landing would look, over which commentary between the astronauts – now a matter of metres away from the lunar surface – and Mission Control in Houston was relayed. And then the words 'Contact Light', followed by 'OK, engines stop', could be heard being spoken from the surface of the Moon. As cameras cut back to the two men in the studio, Schirra wiped a tear from his eye.

Later that evening, television broadcast the words 'Live from the Moon' as the landscape of this alien world was relayed back to Earth. For the last decade or so, TV had been making the world feel a lot smaller, but for those witnessing the first lunar landing, the universe suddenly felt within reach.

At 10.56pm Eastern Time, Neil Armstrong climbed out of the Lunar Module and became the first human being to set foot on the Moon, shortly followed by Buzz Aldrin. The third member of the crew – Michael Collins – waited in lunar orbit for their return. But as America paused to take in the rewards of their endeavours, they did not do so alone. Across the world, more than 600 million people – one-fifth of the world's population at the time – were watching along.

In London, although it was nearly 3am, huge crowds gathered in front of a TV screen in Trafalgar Square. Elsewhere in the country, children were allowed to stay up late to witness this historical event. Live images of the first steps on the surface of the Moon were beamed by satellites to televisions across the world. From Japan to Kuwait, Australia to Vatican City (where the Pope had stayed up to watch), for a brief moment much of the world stopped, united in awe at what they were witnessing. Even behind the Iron Curtain, Sergei Khrushchev – the son of the former Soviet Premier Nikita Khrushchev – went outside and used a telescope to look up at the Moon.

Although it was American astronauts on the surface, what had happened was bigger than any one nation. Humans were on the Moon and the world was watching. For those brief moments on 20 July 1969, for all the divisions that still existed on Earth, many were united in seeing those first images of people on another world.

To this day, the story of the Apollo 11 Moon landing continues to inspire, even for generations that were born long after. It was a defining moment of human achievement, witnessed by hundreds of millions back on Earth, that changed who we are. The Moon was no longer a companion in our sky but a tangible possibility – an extension of where we could go. And the advances of technology in the twentieth century had made possible not just the feat itself, but for so many to be part of this moment.

Some months after returning from space, the crew of Apollo 11 embarked on a goodwill tour around the world. There they heard cries of 'We did it!' Not, 'America did it!' – 'We did it!' For while the Moon landing was of course a definitive show of US technical supremacy in space, and it was an American flag planted on the lunar surface, what the mission and the crew represented was not just one nation, but instead one species – humans. News coverage had talked of 'Man on the Moon' and the plaque the astronauts left behind on the surface read, 'Here men from the planet Earth first set foot on the Moon.'

But while seeing people on another world briefly united us and inspired so many to this day and most likely beyond, the story of how we got there is not steeped in unity nor wonder and awe, but instead in division. The space race owes its origins to the bloodiest conflict of all time, and it took place against a backdrop of the ongoing threat of all-out nuclear war between two superpowers with deeply conflicting ideologies.

*

The famously audacious challenge to send humans to the Moon (and return them safely to Earth) was laid down by President Kennedy just months after his inauguration.

On 25 May 1961, when the president stood before a joint session of Congress and asked them to commit the funds, the US had just 15 minutes of human spaceflight experience, after astronaut Alan Shepard completed a short space mission, landing a matter of miles from where he had launched. Kennedy also called for new types of rockets, as well as weather and communication satellites. It was the dawn of a new era in exploration.

'Now it is time to take longer strides,' Kennedy told Congress, 'time for a great new American enterprise – time for this nation to take a clearly leading role in space achievement, which in many ways may hold the key to our future on Earth.' Kennedy had convinced them that 'no single space project would be more impressive to mankind' – Congress voted virtually unanimously in favour of America's Moonshot. From that speech, the commitment was made: GO for the Moon.

The United States had by this time been locked in a 'Space Race' with its Cold War enemy the Soviet Union for some years, and when Kennedy made his speech they were losing. This race was not just about scientific achievement; it also represented two superpowers battling to showcase the supremacy of their own ideologies. But it was the Soviets, and not the United Stated as many had expected, who, on 4 October 1957, had launched the first human-made satellite and taken humanity into the Space Age. Named Sputnik (Russian for 'travelling companion'), it was silver and beach-ball-sized, with four spidery antennas, and completed an orbit of our planet in a mere 96 minutes. Radio operators across the world picked up Sputnik's sinister cry of 'beep beep beep'. One reporter described the sound as becoming, in a matter of days, 'as much a part of twentieth-century life as the whirl of your vacuum cleaner'.

While the US focused on plans to send the country's own satellites to space, the reality was the nation had been beaten. Then, less than a month later, the Soviet Union launched Sputnik 2. On board was a passenger, a dog, nicknamed Laika. America hadn't even got a satellite into orbit and the Soviets were sending an animal, a stray dog that they had found on the streets, on a mission where death was certain.

Laika's final home was a padded and windowless space capsule, complete with air conditioning and a feeding system – a much larger and heavier object than Sputnik 1. Her mission was to provide information on the effects of weightlessness on a living creature, as we simply didn't know what would happen to people in these conditions, and sending an animal was considered the only way to find out. The trip was always going to be one way. The technology or know-how to get her back simply didn't exist yet. However, her death was still untimely. Laika died within hours of reaching orbit due to her compartment overheating, but the world was told by the Soviet propaganda machine that Laika was still alive and well for days after launch.

America was slipping further behind in the race, and tensions were rising. The US's first attempt to launch a satellite – Vanguard TV3 – two months after Sputnik, in December 1957, ended in failure. It managed to lift only about four feet from the launchpad before crashing back down and bursting into flames. The American press swiftly christened it 'Flopnik' and 'Kaputnik'. It wasn't until the end of January 1958 that America finally got its first satellite, Explorer 1.

But the claim of being the first country to send a human into space, that was the ultimate prize. And soon, America was introduced to its first astronauts – the Mercury Seven, the team named after the capsule in which they would ride to space. On 9 April 1959, the newly formed space agency NASA (National Aeronautics and Space Administration) introduced a group of seven suited, 30-something men with matching buzz cuts to journalists and television cameras during their first press conference. All were military test pilots, used to flying new and advanced aircraft. The seven men rose to their feet for a round of applause from the waiting media. Their mission would be Project Mercury, the NASA programme to put a person into space, and they would compete with each other for the accolade of being chosen to be the first.

Then, on 12 April 1961, Jules Bergman – a well-known TV science reporter of the era – began his ABC television special report by proclaiming the day as 'one of the most unforgettable of our century'. But it was not an American astronaut, rather a Soviet cosmonaut called Yuri Gagarin who had become the first person to ever travel to space. A 27-year-old Russian had travelled higher, faster and further than any other human to date, and become the first to hold the title of 'space explorer', while America could only look on. The Mercury Seven were left to fight for second place.

News reports in America asked what was next for the Soviet Union; their victory in sending the first person to space was described as a 'triumph of Soviet science over the West'. The smiling photograph of Yuri Gagarin, which had been released to the US media, quickly became as familiar as their country's own soon-to-be astronauts. For many, the fear was that if their Cold War enemy, the Soviet Union, was to continue to dominate in space, what would this mean for their lives on Earth?

It was undeniable that when it came to the feat of leaving and orbiting around our planet, the Soviet Union was ahead. And so if America was to show dominance in space, it was not going to be able to do so close to Earth. Instead, President Kennedy was advised that if the US was to stand a chance in demonstrating its technological superiority, then the Moon would be a more 'even playing field'. When Kennedy made his speech in 1961, NASA had not yet developed a rocket powerful enough to get humans that far, but intelligence had shown that neither had the Soviets. By changing the direction of the Space Race, America had a chance of winning.

But by making the commitment to a mission to the Moon, Congress had bound the American people to what would become the most expensive civilian project in the history of the country. If the Moonshot was to succeed, it was necessary not just to develop new technology, but also to convince the public that it was possible. So, on a bright and humid September day in Houston, Texas, on the campus of Rice University, President Kennedy stood before some 40,000 people. It had been more than a year since Congress had given the go-ahead, but it was now time to lay out the rallying cry for the nation. 'We choose to go to the Moon,' Kennedy told his rapt audience. 'We choose to go to the Moon in this decade and do the other things, not because they are easy, but because they are hard.' It would become one of the most famous speeches ever given by a president.

For the audience in Texas, but also crucially for the TV audience at home, President Kennedy painted a picture of successful endeavours of human exploration and knowledge, and of just how much possibility lay before us. And perhaps most importantly, he made it clear to the American people that if they were willing to accept this challenge, then it would be 'one we intend to win'. A nation cheered. Five days later, a second group of astronauts – dubbed the New Nine - were introduced on screen to the public, and the journey to the Moon began.

Even Kennedy's assassination didn't detract from the Moonshot. It could even be argued that his untimely demise at the age of 46 helped to fuel this ambition, a way for the nation to live out the slain president's promise – his words no longer a rallying cry but a higher calling. For all of the turmoil of the sixties, the promise of the Moon provided hope for some.

In the year of President Kennedy's death, the Soviet Union had become the first to send a woman – former textile worker Valentina Tereshkova – into space. And its cosmonaut Alexei Leonov would, on 18 March 1965, become the first person to perform a spacewalk – floating free of his spacecraft attached by a tether with just his spacesuit protecting him from the unwelcoming void of space. Meanwhile, America continued trying to play catch up – even though the challenge of the Moon had never been publicly accepted by those behind the thick veil of the Iron Curtain.

In fact, very little was known about the Soviet space efforts, but news reports still sometimes speculated as to what they might be doing next, which in turn would drive both fear and patriotism in America. NASA's efforts – both success and failures – were continually played out in the media, with the country's astronauts depicted as heroes, frequently gracing the covers of magazines, appearing on television and making public appearances. This was exactly what Americans needed – heroes and displays of what the country could achieve – as tensions with the Soviets and their allies grew.

But while the astronauts were by now celebrities and, most importantly, 'all-American heroes', one of the masterminds behind the US space programme was not: Wernher von Braun was in many ways the opposite. A German and a former member of the Nazi Party, von Braun was a very unlikely candidate for the spotlight during this time of intense national fervour in the USA. But his passion for space travel became almost as familiar to US audiences as the swagger of their space travellers.

Von Braun had come to America after the Second World War as part of Operation Paperclip – a secret programme that brought some 1,600 German scientists, engineers and technicians to the United States, following the collapse of Nazi Germany. In the affidavit that von Braun had to sign as part of his surrender, he stated that he had rejected the ideology of Hitler but had joined the Nazi Party because refusing to do so would have meant giving up his life's work in rocket engineering. Working in Germany, he had masterminded the V-2, the world's first long-range guided ballistic missile. This weapon of terror had brought devastation to already traumatised cities such as London, Paris and Antwerp, and was responsible for killing thousands in the final years of the conflict. Travelling faster than the speed of sound, unlike with previous bombings, there was no warning of the rocket's approach – instead, those on the ground only heard it after it struck. The V-2s were built underground using workers from concentration camps – of whom more died while constructing these than did at the receiving end of the rockets in Allied cities. To what extent von Braun knew about this has never been clear.

Neither the Americans nor the Soviet Union had this technology, but both countries – who had fought on the same side during the conflict – wanted it. In the wake of the surrender of Nazi Germany, the uneasy union between these nations had begun to unravel, and they grappled to develop similar technological capabilities.

However, the power of the V-2 extended beyond the horrors it inflicted. Launched vertically before travelling at speeds of up to 3,500 miles per hour, this was also the first space rocket – though one that carried nearly a tonne of explosives. It could travel to heights of up to 62 miles, to the edge of space, before bringing terror and destruction on Earth. The genius of von Braun – enabled by the darkness of war and the vengeance of the Nazis in a last-ditch attempt to avoid surrender – had taken humanity into the Space Age.

Gaining von Braun – over the Soviet Union, who also had their own secret operation to gather Nazi German experts – had been a real coup for the Americans. With him came access to this new technology, which could be developed not only as a weapon, but also to provide entry to space, as scientists looked for the first time at the technical feasibility of exploration beyond Earth. The thinking in this Cold War era was that the nation that could access space would have technological dominance on Earth.

Upon arriving in the US, von Braun, along with many other Nazi scientists and engineers, worked for the US Army and later NASA (which would be created in 1958). But American TV audiences got to know von Braun not for the dark history he was a part of, but instead for his passion for space. Appearing alongside Walt Disney, von Braun – who as a child had been fascinated by space and inspired by the writers Jules Verne and HG Wells – used the platform of television, and the millions of Americans it had the potential to reach, to inspire viewers about the possibilities of space travel. Facing the nation in a suit with his dark hair slicked back, he talked enthusiastically of sending humans to space, then to the Moon and the planet Mars.

Von Braun's influence extended not only to the development of US rockets and the inspiration of a new generation, but to US policy. It was he had who advised President Kennedy's team of the feasibility of beating the Soviets in a race to the Moon. Seeing humans on the lunar surface was a dream that he had had since childhood, at a time when the possibilities of space were still seen as science fiction. So while President Kennedy had inspired the American people to go to the Moon, the idea itself was the vision of von Braun.

With the project to land humans on the Moon underway, von Braun's focus was on leading the development of a rocket which would be capable of taking astronauts to the lunar surface. But in order to succeed in a mission there, what was needed was more than a rocket. NASA needed to know how astronauts could survive in space for longer than just hours and they needed to master skills such as spacewalking, as well as rendezvous and docking two spacecraft.

*

Walter Cronkite sat in his studio before TV audiences on a Sunday morning in December 1965 and introduced the day 'as the most exciting in space'. It was on this day that America was hoping to overtake the Soviet Union in spaceflight.

Through its Gemini programme that year, NASA had started sending two astronauts into space instead of one. Less than three months after Alexei Leonov had become the world's first spacewalker, Ed White had become the first American to spacewalk. Then, in August 1965, astronauts Pete Conrad and Gordon 'Gordo' Cooper had spent eight days in space, more time than any other humans to date – including the Soviets.

As the clock in front of Walter Cronkite's desk counted down to launch, he described the events that were about to unfold. In orbit already were two astronauts, the crew of Gemini 7, who had been living cramped inside their tiny spacecraft for a week. Today's launch, of Gemini 6, would see another crew making their way into space. The aim: to perform the first rendezvous of two crewed spacecraft while in orbit.

This might not sound as historic or as glamorous as the first human flight, but learning how to meet with another craft in space was essential for going to the Moon, and it had never been done before. As Cronkite explained it to those watching at home: 'If we cannot prove the rendezvous technique, we do not have the means of getting a man back off the Moon after putting him there.'

Plans for the Apollo programme, which would follow the Gemini missions, involved landing two astronauts on the surface of the Moon in a smaller craft called the Lunar Module (or LM for short – pronounced 'lem'), while a third astronaut remained in orbit in the larger Command and Service Module. After leaving the lunar surface, the LM would need to meet up and dock with the Command and Service Module in orbit around the Moon. Not only that, but, Cronkite explained, 'Being able to meet up with another craft is essential for future plans for an orbiting space station, as well as having the potential to rescue future stranded astronauts.' Success would mark a huge technological milestone.

It's easy to describe, but the act of rendezvous with another craft in space is so complex that at one point it was thought it might not be possible. In the strange environment of orbit, if you speed up, that action takes you to a higher orbit, which in turn slows you down. And if you slow down, you are taken to a lower orbit, which in turn speeds you up. It goes against everything pilots would do on Earth, and the calculations to do this required some of the brightest minds at the time.

As the clock struck T-minus 30 seconds, the coverage cut to live images from Cape Canaveral in Florida as NASA continued the countdown. On 'zero', the rocket roared to life, a cloud of smoke forming beneath it, as it prepared to take the crew away from Earth. But it did not take off. Instead, the engine shut down. And the rocket remained on the launchpad – the result of a technical problem. Those watching on would have to wait to see America overtake the Soviets.

Three days later Gemini 6 did successfully launch. In orbit around our planet, the spacecraft was able to catch up with Gemini 7 – the crew of which had by now spent ten days cramped in their tiny spacecraft. The two craft did not actually dock – the mission had not been designed to do that – but they came within just 30 centimetres of each other. Two spacecraft flying side by side in space, almost like aircraft in formation. The year closed with the Americans having succeeded in doing something the Soviet Union had never done before, as they inched ahead in the space race. To those looking on in the West, a friendly Moon felt a little closer.

*

While von Braun was a public figure in the US, the mastermind behind the Soviet space programme remained largely unknown. Even behind the Iron Curtain, it is claimed, some of the cosmonauts who would ride on the rockets he had designed – entrusting their lives to his creations – knew him only as 'Chief Designer'. It was a policy of secrecy that had begun with Stalin and continued under the leaders who followed him – one that claimed to provide protection from assassination attempts by the West.

But in January 1966, the father of Soviet rocketry, the

Soviet Union's chief designer, died. At his state funeral on a frigid winter's day in Moscow, crowds looked on as Sergei Korolev's remains were enshrined within the walls of the Kremlin. There was a smiling photograph of a middle-aged man with a round face, dark hair and medals pinned to his chest lying among a sea of flowers. With the mourners stood Yuri Gagarin, Valentina Tereshkova and Alexei Leonov. These famed cosmonauts were now left orphans of their own space programme. It had been Sergei Korolev who had been responsible for so much of the success of the Soviet Union in space.

At the time, news of the death of Korolev did not make headlines around the world, as so few were aware of exactly how much he had achieved. However, details of his life slowly began to emerge. A brilliant manager, he was said to be an obsessive worker who apparently slept for only a few hours a night. He and his team of engineers had dissected the V-2s that had been captured after Nazi Germany surrendered and used them to develop Soviet rockets. It was under his leadership that the Soviet Union had become the first to orbit a satellite, a living creature and then a person.

Born in Zhitomir, today part of Ukraine, Korolev was a qualified pilot who had studied aeronautics in Moscow, where he designed gliders to which he would add rocket engines. Though loyal to the Soviet system, he became one of the many academics and intellectuals who were caught up in the Great Purges of Joseph Stalin in the late 1930s; he was beaten, arrested and imprisoned at one of the most notorious gulags. Here, Korolev would serve just a matter of months before being transferred to a prison in Moscow. However, that was long enough in these horrendous conditions for the young engineer to be left with a broken jaw and no teeth.

It was after the Americans gained von Braun, following the surrender of Nazi Germany, that Korolev's life had a change of luck. He was sent to work first on the captured V-2s and then to develop the capabilities to send a satellite into orbit. By the beginning of 1966, Sergei Korolev had been leading the world in the exploration of space for a decade. Now he was gone.

Following Korolev's death – on the operating table, during what was expected to be a routine surgery – the Soviet Union had no choice but to carry on in their quest to journey into space without him. But for the rest of the year the Soviet Union did not send a single cosmonaut to space, while the US continued to celebrate the success of its Gemini programme, finessing the skills of rendezvous, docking and spacewalking.

Many watching on in America felt like their fortunes in the space race were changing. While there had been losses – most notably astronauts Charlie Bassett and Elliot See, who had been killed in a plane crash – as well as near misses, when a then unknown astronaut by the name of Neil Armstrong had had to abort the flight of Gemini 8 after the spacecraft began spinning out of control, a quick-thinking move that saved his life and that of fellow astronaut Dave Scott – America was still making steady progress. For many, the start of 1967 brought about hope that reaching the Moon was now possible.

The first Apollo mission, dubbed Apollo 1, had been scheduled for launch in February 1967. But late into the evening of 27 January 1967, television programmes were interrupted with a special report that brought the growing optimism to a halt.

'This is a time for great sadness. But it is also a time for courage, and if that sounds trite, I'll change the words to guts,' said Walter Cronkite, as he provided an assessment of the day's events at NASA. 'This program was bound to claim victims. It should not be a cause for us turning back or having any question of faltering.'

America's first three Apollo astronauts – Gus Grissom, Ed White and Roger Chaffee – had been killed by a fire inside their spacecraft earlier that evening. They died not during a launch or in space, but in a routine simulation on the launchpad at Cape Canaveral in Florida. The solemn-looking anchor continued, 'Certainly it shouldn't in any way damage the nation's resolve to press on with the program for which these men gave their lives.' But, he conceded, 'There will be delays.'

Apollo 1 was intended to be the first crewed mission of the programme, testing out the Command and Service Module (needed to take humans to the Moon) in orbit around the Earth. Instead, just at the point when the Moon had felt within reach, it seemed to many watching on that it was slipping away. As the nation buried its astronauts, colleagues at NASA – despite their resolve to continue

– were unsure if they were burying three men or the entire space programme.

While America tried to recover from the aftermath of Apollo 1, the Soviet Union was also in mourning. In late April, the charred remains of cosmonaut Vladimir Komarov were displayed during his open-casket funeral. Like Korolev before him, his ashes were interred in the walls of the Kremlin. The cosmonaut's Soyuz spacecraft had been plagued with faults and its parachute failed to deploy on re-entry, causing it to plummet to Earth. He was killed instantly. The desire to reach space had costs lives on both sides. Although this wasn't a war, it was a rivalry with a human cost.

It would take until the second half of 1968 for both American astronauts and Soviet cosmonauts to return to space. After un-crewed tests, Apollo 7 was to set to fulfil the promise of the ill-fated Apollo 1. But this time there was more of an air of uncertainty that hadn't been felt before – NASA was still reeling from the loss of its first Apollo astronauts; any further accidents and it could lose the race for the Moon.

But Apollo 7 succeeded in its mission and America was back into space, once again focused on the Moonshot, as the close of the decade inched closer. But being first was still not guaranteed.

Just a month earlier, the Soviet Union had reached their own milestone, successfully sending a craft into orbit around the Moon and returning it safely to Earth. The onboard crew of two tortoises unknowingly became the first living creatures from Earth to travel around the Moon. Along with the animal cargo were fruit fly eggs, cells of wheat, barley, peas and specimens of wildflowers, included to test the effect of exposure to cosmic radiation on terrestrial biology. While America celebrated their return to human spaceflight, there was now speculation that the Soviets could be just months away from sending a person to the Moon.

It was not originally planned that the next Apollo mission – Apollo 8 – would fly to the Moon. Instead, it would be testing out the Lunar Module (LM) for the first time while orbiting the Earth. This four-legged contraption had no seats for astronauts as it was designed to be as lightweight as possible – parts of the craft were as thin as a few sheets of tin foil. Apollo 8's mission was to fly this new type of spacecraft and practise the complex techniques needed to dock and undock with the Command and Service Module. In other words, testing out all the procedures needed for a lunar landing, but in the familiarity of Earth orbit.

To land astronauts on the Moon, the Apollo spacecraft had three parts known as the Command Module, Service Module and Lunar Module. After launch, the Command and Service Module would dock with the Lunar Module and they would travel to lunar orbit together as one spacecraft. Once in orbit around the Moon, the Lunar Module would undock, carrying the two astronauts who would land it on the surface while the third astronaut remained alone in the Command and Service Module. The upper half of the Lunar Module would then take off from the Moon, using the lower half as a launchpad. After reuniting with the Command and Service Module, the Lunar Module would be jettisoned. Just before re-entry to the Earth's atmosphere, the Service Module would also be jettisoned, leaving just the Command Module, which was equipped with a heat shield to enable it to return to Earth with the crew. It was an incredibly complex operation, which is why the first Apollo missions were never designated to go straight to the Moon.

But it became clear that the LM was not going to be ready and there was a growing fear that the Soviets were pulling ahead. So, just five weeks before it launched, NASA made the bold call that Apollo 8 would become the first crewed mission to fly around the Moon. It was a daring move, one that the crew would later admit had only a 50–50 chance of success. Failure would mean that, with little more than a year until the close of the decade, it would be unlikely America would succeed in reaching President Kennedy's goal. For the families of the three astronauts – Frank Borman, Bill Anders and Jim Lovell – the return of their loved ones was not guaranteed.

Not only would the crew attempt to become the first humans to travel around another world in our solar system, they would launch atop von Braun's behemoth rocket, the Saturn V, the largest, most powerful rocket ever built. It had been launched twice on crewless test flights – the first of which had been a success, the second had malfunctioned. Everything about this mission was risky. But succeeding in orbiting around the Moon and returning safely to Earth would put America on course for a lunar landing in 1969.

On the day of launch – 21 December – families across America and much of the world once again gathered around their televisions to watch the next spectacle in the race for the Moon. On the Space Coast of Florida – the area around the Kennedy Space Center – crowds flocked to get a glimpse of the 111-metre-high Saturn V rocket as it took off in the distance.

As the sun rose, the Saturn V came to life. The most powerful rocket ever built began to tear through the sky. Its roar was so loud that news cameras shook; even the building the reporters were stationed in three miles away began to shake. The flames beneath the Saturn V were so bright that from a distance of a few miles – the closest you could get to the launch – it resembled a giant firework. Among those looking on was Wernher von Braun, the rocketry mastermind, now in his late fifties, his dark hair now a white-grey. He watched as his creation – one he had dreamt of since childhood – began its voyage to the Moon.

Over the coming three days – the time it would take to get to the Moon – ABC science reporter Jules Bergman, joined by news anchor Frank Reynolds, greeted audiences from their space-age studio, complete with a model of the Moon and the Earth behind them. A ticker on screen counted up the distance in miles that Apollo 8 had so far travelled away from Earth. There, they introduced the first TV pictures from the crew – grainy footage that showed the astronauts floating inside their spacecraft halfway between the Moon and the Earth, further than any humans had ever ventured before, far enough away that they could see the whole Earth when they looked back. A nation was captivated.

After reaching the Moon and spending 20 hours orbiting it, the crew returned home, splashing down in the Pacific Ocean just six days after launch. Apollo 8 had succeeded in its mission. In doing so, America had leaped from mostly being the underdog to becoming the clear leader in the race for supremacy in space. As the world looked to a new year, the final year of the decade, putting humans on the lunar surface was now firmly within reach for the United States.

The first half of 1969 saw the crew of Apollo 9 test out the Lunar Module in Earth orbit before the crew of Apollo 10 returned to the Moon – not to land on the surface, but to perform a dress rehearsal: undocking the LM from the Command and Service Module, flying it to a distance of little more than nine miles from the lunar surface, then rendezvousing with the Command and Service Module, before returning home. The purpose was to test all the components and procedures ahead of an actual lunar landing.

Both missions succeeded, meaning the next – Apollo 11 – was to be the first to attempt to land humans on the Moon. A moment of reckoning for a nation that had strived to fulfil President Kennedy's words to, 'land a man on the Moon, and return him safely to Earth'.

The crew consisted of Michael Collins, 38, a former Air Force test pilot and the first person to ever spacewalk twice; Buzz Aldrin, 39, a former Air Force pilot, who held a doctorate from MIT in orbital rendezvous, and Neil Armstrong, 38, a former naval aviator and test pilot who, growing up, had learnt to fly before he could drive. Both Buzz Aldrin and Michael Collins had had their initial astronaut applications rejected, and commander Neil Armstrong had experienced little more than ten hours of spaceflight time.

Why were these three men selected? You could say that along with their qualifications, temperament and skills as pilots, there was also some luck involved. As Michael Collins would say in the years after the mission, they all happened to be born at the right time – 1930 – which made them the right age in the sixties to be involved in the space programme. There was also an element of luck to the crew rotations at NASA, which meant they were the astronauts lined up for this mission. But ask any astronaut of the era and they will all say that Neil Armstrong – arguably the greatest pilot that has ever lived – was the right man for the job of commander.

On 20 July 1969, the world looked on with wonder as astronauts Neil and Buzz achieved what for so long had been deemed impossible, and landed on the surface of the Moon. As they looked through the windows of their Lunar Module – which had been named *Eagle* – they could see the ink-black sky and the rocky grey terrain around them. Our planet's satellite, so familiar to us in our night sky, was revealed as an alien world to them. Neil and Buzz spent a total of 21 hours and 36 minutes on the Moon. Their historic Moonwalk lasted just two and a half hours; the rest of their time was spent inside their tiny craft – resting following the landing and then sleeping after the Moonwalk. The pair didn't just walk on the Moon – for just less than an Earth day, they called it their home.

Above them, Michael Collins orbited alone. For all the hundreds of millions watching the landing, Michael was not among them. There was no TV in the Command and Service Module (which had been named *Columbia*). Instead, when *Columbia*'s orbit took him on the near side of the Moon, in range of radio transmissions, he was able to listen in to the historic moment he had been pivotal in creating. While on the far side of the Moon, for 48 minutes of each orbit, he was alone in the darkness, cut off from every single human, with no way of communicating. But he was not lonely. Instead, away from sunlight, he was accompanied by a universe awash with stars.

After lifting off from the lunar surface, Neil and Buzz once again joined Michael, and together the crew began their three-day voyage home to Earth. Those hours spent at the Moon would define the astronauts for the rest of their lives. For Buzz, his life would take some difficult turns – including alcoholism, depression and a stint working as a used car salesman, before he found his passion in inspiring future generations to continue to explore space and to send humans to Mars. As the first person to ever set foot on the Moon, Neil Armstrong became one of the most famous humans that has ever existed. It was a heavy burden to carry for a shy man of few words who did not seek public attention. After Apollo, he would spend hours every day signing autographs. He eventually returned to his first passion – flying – and avoided the limelight.

When Apollo 11 safely splashed down back on Earth on 24 July 1969, President Kennedy's goal had been achieved. Humans had travelled to the Moon and returned safely to Earth, and they had done so with more than five months to spare before the close of the decade. Even in the Soviet Union, the newspapers covered the historic moment, though not with the fervour of other international media. The space race had been won.

The year 1969 drew to a close with a 'whoopie' from astronaut Pete Conrad as he became the third human to walk on the Moon as commander of Apollo 12. His first words on the surface: 'Whoopie! That may have been a small one for Neil, but that was a long one for me' – a play on Neil Armstrong's famous words as he first stepped onto the surface of the Moon: 'One small step for (a) man, one giant leap for mankind.'

In the span of a decade, our world and the universe around us had become smaller, and through television and the advances of space-based technology almost anyone could take in the adventure. In just over eight years, humans had gone from the first crewed space flight to walking on the Moon. We had, to quote the poet John Gillespie Magee Jr, 'Slipped the surly bonds of Earth'.

*

Going to the Moon changed us. Our companion for an eternity; ever-present across centuries of poetry, love stories, wonder and dreams, it was always beyond reach. But in those moments when Neil Armstrong and Buzz Aldrin landed on the lunar surface, we were no longer bound to one world. In a universe vast beyond the imagination, we took our first step away from our home. All those born after this moment, myself included, would never know a time when a piece of our sky had not been claimed by humanity. Today we look to the Moon and know it is no longer a place to dream of, but a place we have begun to explore.

In total there were six crewed landings on the Moon – Apollos 11, 12, 14, 15, 16 and 17 – and a total of 12 astronauts walked on its surface. Apollo 13 did not land; instead it narrowly averted disaster during the journey, and the survival of the crew was due to the quick thinking and determination of the team at NASA's Mission Control.

In December 1972, NASA prepared to launch what would be its final mission to the land on the Moon – Apollo 17. With the space race won, coupled with the huge costs of going to the Moon, there was no justification to continue. From his studio, built on the Press Site at the Kennedy Space Center, Walter Cronkite introduced an interview with Wernher von Braun. Now retired from NASA, the engineer talked optimistically of a return to the

Moon, which he expected to happen within the next ten years. He likened Apollo to the 'sailing ship and dog-sled era to the South Pole' – the first missions to a new land, which were succeeded by more advanced technology that enabled people to go further. Even with public enthusiasm for spaceflight waning, von Braun said he was 'not pessimistic' for the future of space exploration and talked of his hope of seeing astronauts landing on the Moon's surface using the reusable Space Shuttle, which NASA had by then begun developing.

Five years later, von Braun died of pancreatic cancer. The last time humans were on the surface of the Moon was 14 December 1972. In an interview in 2019, his younger daughter Margrit – herself a scientist – talked of how, if he were still alive today, her father would be disappointed not only that we have not returned to the Moon, 'but that we have not been to Mars'. Margrit explained that as soon as Apollo launched, her father had begun talking about how to get humans further into space.

Today, a bust of von Braun stands outside NASA's Marshall Space Flight Center in Huntsville, Alabama, where he worked to create the rocket which would take humans to the Moon. His connection to the Nazi Party in the Second World War means his standing in history is not without controversy, but his place in the development of space exploration is indisputable.

To those who worked for him, his vision gave him almost god-like status. I once interviewed one of the German rocket scientists who had travelled to America to work with von Braun. To him, he was a hero, and the story of the work they did to send Americans into space so powerful that it brought him to tears. They, and the many others who worked with him in America, felt that under his guidance they were pursuing something greater – working to create the machines that would take humans from this Earth.

As for the Soviet Union, they never did land a human on the Moon. And for a long time it wasn't clear if the Soviets had even been planning to. Could the race for the Moon have been a paranoid delusion of the Americans? At the start of 1969, the Soviets had docked two crewed vehicles in orbit around the Earth, in a technique like that used by the Americans, which was necessary for a lunar landing. But all of their human spaceflight missions that year instead focused on Earth orbit. Any ambitions for the Moon were cloaked in secrecy.

Years later it would be discovered that they were indeed racing the Americans to the Moon. In 1989, the *New York Times* revealed that engineers from MIT (Massachusetts Institute of Technology) on a visit to Moscow had become the first from the West to see the Soviet Lunar Lander. Metallic copper in colour, it featured a round space capsule at the top, with a docking hatch above a radio antenna and legs for landing on the Moon. The Soviets had built it, but it had never flown.

After America won the space race, the Soviet Union focused on robotic missions; a month after Apollo 11, their spacecraft Zond 7 orbited the Moon. Although there were no cosmonauts onboard, it contained a mannequin with the face of Yuri Gagarin cast onto it. The first person to travel into space, Yuri Gagarin had died in a plane crash a year earlier, at the age of 34. While no cosmonaut from the Soviet Union would ever get to see the Moon up close, the mask of Gagarin represented the spirit of the nation in space.

One of the reasons for the Soviet Union's failure to win the space race lay in the design of its rocket, the N1. Designed by Soviet mastermind Sergei Korolev, the gigantic 100-metre-tall device was his hope of getting cosmonauts to the Moon. However, Korolev could not come to an agreement with some of his team about the types of engines to use, and development of the rocket was put on hold until 1964. By 1968, the nation was ready to go to the Moon but Korolev was dead, and repeated failed launch attempts without him delayed the programme, eventually seeing it cancelled in the early 1970s.

Had Korolev not died on that operating table in 1966, would the results have been the same? We will never know, but the great rocket pioneer's legacy lives on: the Soyuz spacecraft, which to this date is the most successful spacecraft ever built and regularly launches space travellers from across the world, is his design. Korolev took the first human to space, and many of those who make the journey today do so because of his legacy.

Although the success of Apollo 11 technically ended the space race, it would take a handshake in 1975 to change the way we saw space from a place of rivalry to a place for co-operation. 'The hatch has closed on two days of what has been Soviet–American harmony in space, something that has escaped the two nations on Earth,' announced Walter Cronkite in a CBS News special report.

By now, more people had colour televisions than black-and-white ones. The footage showed two smiling cosmonauts floating in their navy-blue flight suits as the door separating their Soyuz spacecraft from the American Apollo spacecraft was shut. First in Russian and then in English, the crew said 'наша следующая встреча вернется на землю' – 'our next meeting would be back on Earth'.

This meeting in space marked a policy of détente between the two superpowers, in a bid to improve relations that had begun to develop in the years since Apollo 11 landed on the Moon. Just as space had been a very visible stage for supremacy, now that stage was being used for a show of unity. Each spacecraft had been specifically designed to dock with the other in orbit, before spending two days bound together. The American NASA astronauts – Tom Stafford, Deke Slayton (a member of the Mercury Seven, who had finally made it to space) and Vance Brand – had learned to speak Russian for the mission. And the two Soviet cosmonauts – Alexei Leonev (the world's first space-walker) and Valeri Kubasov – had learned English. As the hatch separating the two spacecraft opened, commanders Alexei Leonev and Tom Stafford met in the middle and shook hands. A new way of doing space had begun.

Over the coming 48 hours, the two crews worked side

by side. They conducted medical experiments and even tried each other's food. Cronkite's CBS special report broadcast a tour of the Soyuz, filmed by astronaut Vance Brand, as cosmonaut Valeri Kubasov proudly showed off his nation's spacecraft. The cosmonaut then brought out a photograph to show the cameras – a picture of him with his wife and two children. For so long the Soviet Union had been the enemy, but when it came to it, what they cared about most was exactly the same as the American people.

Then some words appeared on the film, which, to those watching at home, would have once seemed almost as ludicrous as the notion of seeing the surface of the Moon broadcast live into their living rooms: the caption 'USSR from Space' flashed up as the video camera pointed out of the window and looked back at the country. 'There is nothing more beautiful than our blue planet,' cried Kubasov, as he guided viewers through the sights below him. Later they passed over the cloud-covered east coast of the United States; below them was North Carolina and the site of Kitty Hawk, where the world's first aeroplane had flown just 72 years prior. In less than the timeframe of one human lifetime, we had gone from a flight that lasted just seconds to two conflicted nations working together in space.

As the tapes from space ended, Walter Cronkite finished his special report with a question to viewers: 'Where will it lead …?'

Twenty-three years later, construction on the International Space Station (ISS) began, as a collaboration between 16 countries, including the United States and what is now Russia. It is the largest human-made object ever constructed in orbit and a project that many think is deserving of the Nobel Peace Prize – the criteria of which include fraternity between nations and the promotion of peace. Aboard the ISS we are at peace – even countries which may be divided by politics or ideologies on Earth co-operate in orbit around our planet to tackle the huge hurdles we face in exploring space. In humanity's only off-world outpost, we work together harmoniously for the benefit of us all.

In the years since Apollo–Soyuz, space slowly shifted from being a place of conflict and competition to somewhere we are united in pursuing the many benefits that can come from leaving Earth. Today, when astronauts from many countries (not just America) go to space, they learn Russian as part of their training, and Russians must speak English. Though it would be naive to say there is a completely harmonious front in space (there are of course military satellites used by many nations across the world), much of what we do in science and human spaceflight relies on international collaboration.

The Apollo–Soyuz project didn't end the Cold War, but what it did show was that two countries divided by ideology and suspicious of each other's actions are capable of working together in space. The cost had been huge for both nations – $250 million each in 1975 ($3–4 billion in today's money). But what it represented was even more significant: not just an abandonment of competition on

Earth but also a pledge to share the huge costs of pushing further into space, as well as the rewards to come from doing so – something that is essential if we are to continue to explore further.

In America, after Apollo–Soyuz there was a halt to human spaceflight, until the Space Shuttle first launched in 1981. This was a new type of space vehicle that, unlike all earlier spacecraft, was designed to be fully reusable, taking off like a rocket and then returning to Earth flying through the sky like a glider as it slowed down, before landing on a runway. Both the orbiter – the part where the crew sat, which resembled an aeroplane – and the two solid rocket boosters could be serviced and then reused after every mission.

Meanwhile, the Soviet Union's focus on human missions shifted to space stations. The masterpiece of Soviet engineering was Mir, which in the late 1980s and early 1990s, before the ISS, was the largest human-made object in space. However, when the Soviet Union crumbled in 1991, the cosmonauts on board were left to return to a very different country.

But it was the fall of the Soviet Union that opened the door to further co-operation between the two nations in spaceflight. Mir would go on to play host to more than 100 cosmonauts and astronauts – with both the Space Shuttle and the Soyuz docking with the Space Station as the two countries began working together in space regularly. In 2011, when the shuttle retired, NASA astronauts began to ride to space aboard the Russian Soyuz. Citizens of two nations once on the brink of all-out nuclear war, and still sharing an edge of suspicion, were sitting side by side to journey beyond Earth.

Today, space exploration is the preserve of more than just two nations. Countries including China, India, France, the United Kingdom and Brazil, to name but a few, have their own space programmes. Many countries have their own national astronauts and there is international involvement in the many robotic missions which are exploring our wider solar system, uncovering worlds that humans cannot yet reach. Going into space is now truly global. Even getting humans to space involves collaboration – there are only three countries on Earth that have the capabilities to launch people: the United States, Kazakhstan (the launch site there, Baikonur, is leased to the Russians) and China.

The birth of our Space Age was an incredible time of progress, but while it is easy to romanticise the era, the reality is that it was driven by conflict and competition. However, in the end it united us, and we know now that in order to continue to explore space we have to do something which often eludes us on Earth: work together.

Thanks to television (and communications satellites in orbit), an entire planet came along for the adventure of our first steps beyond Earth. Today, we are all able to access space through the technology readily available to many of us on the planet, from the birth of stars imaged by the Hubble Space Telescope, to a live broadcast of astronauts orbiting above us aboard the ISS. The intertwining of various technical capabilities means the universe is just a click of a button away in the palm of your hand.

And while the Moon landings were the greatest feat of human technological ingenuity to date, what the birth of space exploration really taught us is that when we go to space we do so as citizens of planet Earth. When you next look up at the Moon in the night sky, consider this: on its surface there is a piece of art left by the crew of Apollo 15 – a small metallic spaceman lying face down next to a plaque that lists the name of every American astronaut and Soviet cosmonaut that lost their lives in the space race. In our pursuit of the stars, we are all on the same team.

Chapter Two

DEDICATION, DETERMINATION AND SACRIFICE

'This ordinary person is contributing to history.'

Christa McAuliffe

As you walk through the doors to the main office of the Astronauts Memorial Foundation (AMF) in Florida, you are greeted by rows of smiling portraits. Men and women of different races and religions frozen in time, their photographs a stark reminder of the human cost of exploring space.

Just metres away from the AMF offices in the Kennedy Space Center stands the visitors' complex, a place where tourists, basking in the year-round sunshine, can come to soak up our many achievements in space. Located in an area of Florida dubbed the Space Coast, on the shores of the Atlantic Ocean, this is one of the world's few gateways to space. Sprawling over 219 square miles, the Kennedy Space Center is home to much of our past, present and future of space exploration. It is from these shores that humans first left Earth bound for the Moon, where the Hubble Space Telescope – which gave us a new window onto the universe – launched aboard the Space Shuttle and where many of the next generation of space companies look to our future in space. In fact, with the exception of some military test flights in the 1960s using the X-15 – a rocket-powered plane which skimmed the edge of space – and recent commercial tourism trips, every single crewed flight from US soil has launched from here.

The most dominant feature on site is the Vehicle Assembly Building, or VAB for short. It's a colossal building, with the round NASA 'meatball' logo and the largest American flag in the world painted on it. It was constructed in the 1960s as a place to vertically assemble the Saturn V, and its 139-metre-high doors take 45 minutes to open or close. Alongside the VAB is the Launch Control Center. It is from here that Wernher von Braun looked on as the rocket he had masterminded first launched humans to the Moon. Inside, in what is known as the firing room, controllers watch over the initial stages of lift-off before handing over to Mission Control in Houston.

A few hundred metres back is the Press Site, where journalists and TV crews can set up camp during launches. There is a grandstand for viewing, a collection of media buildings and a countdown clock, which stands on the grass in front of the Turn Basin, part of Banana Creek, a body of water which crosses the Kennedy Space Center. The area shares its boundaries with a wildlife reserve, and the press often spot native manatees as they wait for a launch. At three miles from the launchpads, this is the closest viewing site.

Elsewhere is a 2.8-mile long runway that was built to accommodate the landing of the Space Shuttle. And among the many buildings and offices spread out between the green Florida wetlands is the Neil Armstrong Operations and Checkout Building – home to the astronaut crew quarters. It is here that astronauts spend their last night on Earth before eating breakfast (the NASA astronaut tradition being steak and eggs), suiting up, waving to the waiting press and boarding a van to take them to their spacecraft.

It is a hugely historic place – a small part of our world that has enabled us to step beyond our home planet – and a popular tourist attraction. But the Kennedy Space Center has also been the scene of some of the great horrors of space exploration.

Sometimes it can be easy to take for granted all that we have achieved in the past six decades. There have been so many successes. Humans have walked on the Moon, we have photographed far-off galaxies and the birth of stars, and above you right now are up to six humans living and working in orbit aboard the ISS. But our success in space exploration has not come without hardship, and sometimes too has involved the sudden and shocking loss of life.

It was here in Florida that the crew of Apollo 1 died during what was a routine test on the launchpad. Nineteen years later, press, workers, school children and the families of the onboard astronauts watched on speechlessly from the bleachers as the Space Shuttle *Challenger* broke apart shortly after lift-off. And in 2003, families of the crew of the Space Shuttle *Columbia* looked to the runway as the landing clock ticked down to zero to signal the arrival home of the orbiter – and then started counting up. But *Columbia* was not there. Instead the craft had disintegrated during re-entry, with the loss of everyone on board.

To explore takes courage. Astronauts know the dangers. Yet they still choose to continue with their missions, even in the aftermath of such great losses, motivated by that innate curiosity we all have, the experience of leaving our planet and, most importantly, the chance to be a part of opening up a new frontier and using the knowledge gained to benefit all of us on Earth. In many ways, they are pursuing something greater than themselves. What is the risk to one human life when compared to discovering the untold possibilities of the cosmos, to be part of reaching beyond our planet and stepping out into the wider universe?

That is not to say that they do so recklessly. But our exploration beyond Earth is in its infancy. And in leaving our planet we are working at the limit of our technological capabilities. While every effort is made to mitigate risks, they still remain. Riding a rocket is not like flying in a commercial jet or driving a car.

Even if you are not an astronaut, being part of the space industry is not a nine-to-five job. It is a way of life, and it takes enormous dedication. Astronauts may be the public face of exploration, but behind them stand many tens of thousands of people who work on every imaginable aspect of space exploration – from designing spacesuits to building robotic craft and analysing the scientific data that we gather from exploring. Many of them were born with that same yearning to understand what is out there and are willing to dedicate much of their lives to finding out how to make the impossible possible.

But the act of leaving Earth has historically not been

immune to the influences of prejudice and inequality. The decades in which we began to leave Earth saw great changes happening *on* Earth. In its early years, the space industry – like most other professional workplaces in the West – was predominantly 'male and pale'. But it too has benefited from the courage and determination of those who spoke out against discrimination, those who were intent on 'taking their seat at the table' and making sure who *they* are is represented in what humanity does in space. Not all of those who broke down barriers and forged a path necessarily saw themselves as pioneers, but they were all dedicated to the work they were doing; work that is not just a job but a way of life. And they succeeded in spite of the prejudices that would have held them back.

Perhaps most poignantly of all, these stories of our quest to reach beyond Earth are also tales about love and loss. We can learn a lot from our astronauts – not just from their courage, but from their dedication and determination to do something once deemed impossible. But they too are human, with families and loved ones whose lives are impacted by what they have chosen to do.

In a secluded spot in the Kennedy Space Center, out of reach from all but a few, stands the astronauts' beach house. It was here that astronauts would spend time with their families before going into quarantine ahead of their missions. For fourteen families – those of the crews of *Challenger* and *Columbia* – this was the last place that they saw their loved ones alive. Going to space is hard.

Not just for those who face the dangers, but for those they leave behind.

*

During the space race, the high risks associated with human spaceflight were generally accepted. This was a conflict – albeit a silent one – and demonstrating technological supremacy was a new kind of battlefield. The first astronauts were not only decorated military personnel, they were former test pilots – a career that had made them accustomed to burying their colleagues. Mortality rates for pilots flying experimental aircraft rivalled those of wartime. So when it came to the new frontier of space, they faced the risks with gusto and determination – and more than a sprinkle of alpha male competitiveness.

'If we die, we want people to accept it. We are in a risky business, and we hope that if anything happens to us, it will not delay the programme,' astronaut Gus Grissom once famously said. 'The conquest of space is worth the risk to human life.'

Gus Grissom was one of the Mercury Seven – America's first group of astronauts who had been showcased to the world in 1959. Standing at a little over five foot six, with a dark crew cut and a surly manner, Gus might not have appeared to be your typical 'all-American hero', but he was among the best of the best.

Growing up in a small town in Indiana in the 1930s, Gus was an average student from humble beginnings. His family was not wealthy; his father was a railway signalman and his mother a housewife. His early life was marked by a love of the outdoors, and he earned money by working summer jobs picking fruit in the sultry heat of the Midwest. In high school he met a girl called Betty, who became his sweetheart and later his wife.

Yet Gus had something in him that made him determined to work hard and reach for the extraordinary. Having worked as a desk clerk in the military and then for a local bus manufacturer, he enrolled at the prestigious Purdue University. His goal: to become a pilot with the newly formed US Air Force. In order to pay for his studies, he spent 30 hours a week in a diner flipping burgers while his wife Betty worked nights as a telephone operator – meaning he could have evenings alone to study.

Gus succeeded in his ambition and became a decorated war veteran, flying 100 combat missions in Korea. He then worked as an instructor and a test pilot – a role that saw him mastering newly developed fast jets in the desert skies above the prestigious Edwards Air Force Base in southern California. By now, Gus had a reputation of being one of the best 'jet jockeys' in the business, and he received secret orders – along with just 110 others in the country – that he was to be considered for the newly created role of astronaut.

His selection would ultimately see him become the second American – and third person – to ever travel to space. However, his first mission – a 15-minute sub-orbital flight in July 1961 – nearly ended in catastrophe. After splashdown in the Atlantic Ocean, the hatch on his spacecraft – nicknamed *Liberty Bell 7* – blew open prematurely. The ocean began to flood in. Jumping free of the sinking craft, Gus did not have time to close a valve which was used to attach an oxygen pipe to his spacesuit, so it too began to fill with water. He struggled in the churning ocean for five minutes until he was rescued by helicopter. In that time, *Liberty Bell 7* had sunk.

After the mission, Gus was blamed by some – including the media – for what happened. They claimed he had panicked and fired open the door. Some headlines implied – incorrectly – that he had 'flipped the chicken switch'. It was a public humiliation for something he fiercely denied. Unlike many of his peers, he already disliked the attention from the press that being an astronaut brought. The house he would later build for his wife Betty and their two young sons had no street-facing windows so as to keep waiting journalists at bay.

Despite what happened on this initial flight, Gus returned to space, becoming the first person to travel beyond Earth twice, as he commanded the first Gemini mission, along with a then-rookie astronaut, John Young. Poking fun at his previous mishap, they named their spacecraft *Molly Brown*, after the American socialite who had earned the nickname 'the Unsinkable Molly Brown' for her actions during the sinking of the *Titanic*.

By 27 January 1967, Gus was a senior and respected

astronaut at NASA and commander of what was to be the first crewed Apollo mission. Scheduled for launch the following month, it was the kind of mission every test pilot craves. Although they weren't going to the Moon, Gus would get to test out a craft that had never been flown before. As part of preparations for the mission, early that afternoon, he, along with his crew – Ed White, America's first spacewalker and himself a national hero, and a new recruit called Roger Chaffee, who had not yet flown to space – were sealed inside their spacecraft.

The trio were conducting what was known as a 'plugs out' test, which essentially involved doing everything but actually going to space, simulating the procedures during countdown. Wearing their white spacesuits, they took the lift on the red gantry alongside their space rocket and crossed the walkway to get to their spacecraft. There they were strapped to their seats, lying on their backs next to each other, so close that their shoulders were nearly touching. In front of them were their spacecraft control panels, filled with an array of switches. The rocket beneath their spacecraft contained no fuel. Metres away, in the white room attached to the outside of the spacecraft, stood the pad crew – a team whose job it was to support the astronauts.

During a real launch, the gantry with the walkway and the white room would be moved out of the way. But as this was a test, it and the pad crew remained. To reach them, it would take the astronauts 90 seconds to open the three-part hatch of their spacecraft. NASA had considered using one that could be fired open, but after what had happened to Gus on his first mission, they had decided against it, not wanting to put the astronauts at risk.

Inside, the craft was filled with a pure oxygen atmosphere. This was the standard for all US spaceflights. It was a weight-saving technique, which required a lighter environmental control system to pump just one gas into the crew cabin. This was important, because the less a spacecraft weighs, the less fuel is needed to lift it off the ground, which in turn means a reduction in cost. Lighter and simpler trumped heavier and more complicated.

For many hours that afternoon, the crew set to task with the simulated countdown, which was often paused as they dealt with issues. At 6.30pm a frustrated Gus barked, 'How can we get to the Moon if we can't even talk between two or three buildings?' The astronauts were struggling with static noise through the communication systems. In fact, for months Apollo had been plagued with engineering problems – so much so that Gus is said to have hung a lemon on the training simulator as a symbol of his frustration. A crew photo showed them jokingly praying in front of a model of their craft. There were concerns from many of the astronauts – including Gus – that the vehicle was not ready to fly. But time was ticking by, and if President Kennedy's goal was to be met, then project Apollo needed to press on. It was hoped that any issues with the spacecraft could be ironed out before its launch, scheduled for February.

The simulated countdown was paused again so that the

crew and the team over at Mission Control could work on the communication issues. Onsite in Florida, another astronaut, Deke Slayton, looked on through a closed-circuit TV monitor, which pointed towards the spacecraft. Like Gus, Deke was a member of the original Mercury Seven and the two were close friends, but Deke had not yet been to space. He had been grounded because of a minor heart condition and in 1967 he was the director of flight crew operations.

Both managers and astronauts who had been subsequently recruited by NASA thought of Deke as a godfather to the programme. A former Second World War bomber pilot with slightly greying hair, sideburns and pointy ears, he appears in many photographs from the era alongside his more famous counterparts. It was Deke's job to assign crews for missions and, if Gus succeeded as commander of Apollo 1, it was likely that Deke would give him command of the first lunar landing. The boy from a small town in Indiana could be the first to walk on the Moon.

Deke had considered joining the crew that day inside their spacecraft, lying underneath their feet in an attempt to get a better understanding of the issues they had been having, but Gus had decided against it. So instead, Deke watched on the monitors in a blockhouse not far from the launchpad.

At 6.31pm a voice, thought to be Gus's, crackled over the radio. 'Hey … fire,' it said briefly, in a kind of matter-of-fact way. Then another voice, 'We've got a fire in the cockpit.' The static made it impossible to tell whose voice it was. For six seconds only muffled sounds were heard, perhaps movement. Then another voice, thought to be Roger Chaffee, this time more urgent: 'We've got a bad fire.' Then a scream, the kind of blood-curdling scream of pain that makes you sick to your stomach, rising over the crackling of the static noise, followed by silence.

On the closed-circuit TV monitors Deke could see flames spreading from left to right through the window in the spacecraft hatch. Ed White – who was lying in the middle seat –had reached his arm towards the hatch behind him. The pad crew – which consisted of more than 20 men – began battling to prise open the scalding hatch from the outside. But the pure oxygen atmosphere inside the spacecraft was highly pressurised – done to simulate launch conditions – and, as the fire took over, the pressure increased. Then there was a swoosh noise, as the spacecraft ruptured under this enormous pressure and a sheet of flames burst from the craft. It had taken just 18 seconds from the first report of the fire to get to this point.

By now, the black smoke was so thick that the ground crew could barely see the craft. They battled with just two fire extinguishers to calm the flames. As the blaze spread, there was a risk that it could set off the launch escape system on top of Apollo and ignite the entire structure. But the pad crew stayed and continued to fight to get to the astronauts, though many did not have adequate masks to protect them from the smoke and were later treated for smoke inhalation.

At 6.36pm the hatch – which consisted of three parts

– was opened. Four minutes later firefighters arrived, then, at 6.43pm, doctors. Followed shortly after by Deke Slayton.

What greeted them resembled the inside of a furnace. The crew had lost their lives within a matter of seconds of their screams being heard. The cause of death was cardiac arrest, brought on by the toxic fumes in which they were suffocating. Though those final moments for the crew may have been brief, they suffered, the flames having melted away their spacesuits, exposing them to the poisonous environment. Ed and Gus's badly burned bodies were found away from their seats, on the floor. They had tried in vain to open the hatch – an impossible task as it had to be opened inward and the pressure inside was too great. Roger's body was found strapped to his seat – the procedure was for him to remain there communicating with the ground crew until the hatch was open. Just like that, in a matter of seconds, the three astronauts had lost their lives.

The fire had happened on a Friday night and the crew – who had been away all week – had hoped to fly their T-38s home to Houston to see their families that evening. Instead, their wives received the knock on the door that all military spouses dread. While accidents were expected within the space programme, nobody had ever imagined that they would lose a crew on the ground, in a test that had been considered safe.

The investigation into the fire placed blame on a catalogue of errors. Faulty wiring had caused the initial spark.

The fire was then fed by the high-pressure pure oxygen environment and a large amount of flammable materials, such as nylon netting, foam pads and Velcro. The inward-opening hatch, with no firing system to open it quickly, had been rendered impossible to release once the pressure inside the craft had increased – a cruel irony for Gus Grissom, given the mishap of his first spaceflight. All were avoidable mistakes. Working under the time limit imposed by President Kennedy's goal, NASA had been suffering from 'go fever'. Now three astronauts were dead, not in a test flight, nor on a mission, but in an accident on the ground that could so easily have been avoided. Negligent? Yes. But also a failure of imagination – nobody had imagined that so many seemingly obvious mistakes could be made.

For some time, Deke was tormented by the thought that things could have been different had he joined the crew in the command module that day. Perhaps he could have spotted the spark and doused the fire before it spread? He did not know. He described the day as the worst of his life.

In the months after the fire, as the NASA investigation concluded, Deke met with the widows of the crew, who handed him a gift that Gus, Ed and Roger had been saving for him. It was a custom gold astronaut pin, with a diamond in the star. Everyone who is recruited as a NASA astronaut wears a silver astronaut pin – a star shooting through a ring – and when they have flown to space they receive a gold version. The crew had commissioned the pin for Deke as a show of respect – that even though he had not yet gone to space, he was still 'one of them'. The pin stayed with Deke for the rest of his life. He only parted with it once, at the request of Neil Armstrong, who took it with him to the surface of the Moon.

After the investigation, many changes were made to the Apollo spacecraft design, including to the hatch. In fact, all spacecraft to this day – and those being designed for our future – have an outward-opening hatch, which is far less complex and can be fired open in the event of an emergency. This potentially life-saving feature is owed to Gus and the crew of Apollo 1.

In 1999, 30 years to the day after the Apollo 11 Moon landing, Gus Grissom's first spacecraft – *Liberty Bell 7* – was recovered from the depths of the ocean in a salvage mission funded by the Discovery Channel. Unable to find the hatch, they could not prove conclusively what had happened, but the evidence they did uncover suggested it was unlikely Gus had done it. Those who had worked with Gus already believed history had got the story wrong. There was no way that he – a military aviator, test pilot and astronaut of such calibre – would have hit the 'chicken switch'. The recovery of *Liberty Bell 7* helped in some way to vindicate him to others.

When Neil Armstrong and Buzz Aldrin stepped foot on the surface of the Moon on 20 July 1969, they did so because of Gus, along with Ed White and Roger Chaffee. Although Gus never walked on the Moon – as some had suspected he would – the lessons learned from his death helped NASA succeed in getting there, and the subsequent changes to the spacecraft design helped to ensure that no NASA astronauts were lost in space during later Apollo missions. We owe our successes in space to the sacrifices of the crew of Apollo 1. They did not die in vain.

When you go outside and look up at the Moon, Gus, Ed and Roger are there – their names are among those etched onto the plaque left by the crew of Apollo 15, as well as Theodore Freeman, Charlie Bassett, Elliot See, Vladimir Komarov, Edward Givens, Clifton 'C.C.' Williams, Pavel Belyayev, Georgy Dobrovolsky, Viktor Patsayev, Vladislav Volkov and Yuri Gagarin, who lost their lives as we began to reach for space.

Today, the list is sadly a lot longer. In fact, the list of names on the Moon was not even complete at the time – the secrecy of the Soviet Union meant that names were missing. Among them is Valentin Bondarenko, a Soviet cosmonaut whose death bore eerie similarities to those of the crew of Apollo 1 – a fire in a chamber with a high-pressure, high-oxygen atmosphere and an inward-opening door that had been designed not to be easily opened. Both sides in the space race were guilty of the same lack of foresight and imagination.

*

What happened to the crew of Apollo 1 changed NASA. The date, 27 January, is still remembered by the organisation and those within the space industry. The fire made the industry reflect on its 'gung ho' attitude to cutting corners and how things were done. The fact that more could have been done to prevent the Apollo 1 crew members' deaths haunted some of those on the ground for the rest of their lives. 'I can still see the smoke and the flames. I can still hear the cries of my teammates,' wrote one pad worker, 40 years after the fire.

The team at NASA's Mission Control – whose job it is to support space missions from the ground – were left helplessly listening through the radio as the crew died. In the days after the accident, an article in the *New York Times* used the words 'incompetent and negligent' to describe what had happened. The response from NASA Flight Director Gene Kranz was that staff had to become 'tough and competent'.

His speech to the team at Mission Control in the aftermath of the fire laid the blame for the crew's deaths on himself and everyone else who worked there, even though Mission Control was not found by investigators to be at fault. He told his staff that they – himself included – did not do enough: 'We were too gung ho about the schedule … No one stood up and said stop … We were the cause, we were not ready, we did not do our jobs. From this day forward we will be known by two words: tough and competent.'

More than five decades later, 'tough and competent' is still the motto at the core of what it means to work at Mission Control. 'Tough' – because every person should be accountable for what they do, or fail to do; 'competent' – because nothing will be taken for granted; no one should be found short in knowledge and skill. It is a reminder of the very real human cost when mistakes are made in space travel and of the risks taken by those who go there.

As we continue to explore space, the team on the ground works around the clock to make these daring missions possible. And while it may be the astronauts who take the risks, all those who work on a mission bear the brunt of any mistakes that are made. Space exploration is about teamwork. During the height of the space race, more than 400,000 people worked towards the Moon effort. Many of those at NASA – as well as contractor companies – worked hours that matched those of the astronauts, only without the public glory and the fame. It is not much different today, with long hours and shift work.

But so many who work in the space industry choose to work as hard as they possibly can, as long as they possibly can, to further our pursuit of space. During extreme weather events in Houston, staff at NASA's Johnson Space Center, where Mission Control is located, have been known to sleep in the office. The work in space takes priority, no matter what is happening on Earth.

The billionaire Elon Musk once said, 'Nobody changed the world on a 40-hour week.' His company, SpaceX, is notorious for its 80-hour-plus working weeks. Employees sometimes work non-stop at the expense of pretty much everything else in their lives. And yet applications to work at SpaceX far outstrip the number of jobs available. At the heart of the attraction is the knowledge that they are laying the foundations for our species to explore further than ever before. Job adverts for SpaceX explain that they are 'looking for people that want to help us achieve the goal of making humans multi-planetary'. To be a part of something that changes the landscape of what humans are capable of – even if it does not work out as intended – is worth the dedication. It is worth knowing that your short time on Earth was spent pursuing something so incredible. That is what it means to work in the space industry. It is more than 'just a job' – it is a way of life and a way of having an impact on the future of humankind.

*

In 1983, more than 16 years after the fire that had claimed her husband Ed's life, Pat White took her own life. It seems she had never got over his death. While so much is written about the sacrifice and dedication of those who went to space, they were not the only ones who suffered under the stress of pushing forward into this new frontier.

In the 1960s, America's first groups of astronauts became some of the most famous people in the country, if not the world. Behind them stood their wives. At the time, it was NASA's firm belief that their astronauts had to be married. That was a prerequisite for the quintessential all-American hero – he had to be a brave pioneer, a devoted husband and a family man. Divorce was not an option.

And so, in an era long before reality television was conceived, these first astronauts, along with their wives, were in some ways our first reality stars. People wanted to know how the women dressed, how they styled their hair, what they fed their children and how they ran their homes. The public had an almost insatiable appetite for the private lives of the astronauts – perhaps in part as a way of escaping from the ever-growing threat of the Cold War and the turmoil of the era.

With this new-found fame came some money. *Life* magazine struck up a deal – approved by NASA – to pay the Mercury Seven $500,000 (split between them), worth about $4.5 million these days, in exchange for exclusive access. And as more astronaut groups were selected, they too were given similar deals. *Life* magazine even ran a cover with just the wives of the Mercury Seven; inside was an exclusive interview with the women behind the country's first spacemen.

In many ways, their lives seemed idyllic. When their husbands were selected for the programme, the women relocated with them to the comfortable suburbs of Houston, Texas. There, they lived surrounded by the families of other astronauts and staff at NASA. There were often barbecues and parties in this tight-knit space community, and the wives quickly became friends. Once their husbands had been to space, there would be overseas travel, meetings with presidents and world leaders and, of course, beautiful outfits. All of which was photographed and filmed to satisfy the country's ever-growing appetite for these real-life 'supermen' and their families.

But the reality was somewhat different to the stories fed to the public at the time. Their husbands' involvement with the space programme thrust these women into the limelight whether they liked it or not. Their role – at least in public – was to look perfect, smile and support their husbands. But for some it was a heavy burden to bear. During missions, the press would set up camp outside the homes of the astronauts and the women would find them-selves bombarded with questions such as 'Are you scared?' and 'Aren't you worried your husband will be killed?' It was important for the public image of NASA that the astronaut's wife in this situation smiled and showed no fear, though they had little media training or support. The phrase 'proud, happy and thrilled' became the mantra of the women, while they privately wondered if their hus-bands would make it home alive.

It is perhaps a little difficult to be objective when writing about the role of astronauts' wives because today the position of women is very different. But their story needs to be told. In many ways, it was these women who made it possible for the pioneering men to do what they did. The wives of the first astronauts enabled their husbands to think of nothing but the mission. They were their unpaid support systems, running the homes of the astronauts and caring for their children, while facing a life in the public eye that they had not sought and many did not care for.

As the ex-wife of one of the astronauts once put it: 'You think going to the Moon is hard? You ought to try staying at home.'

While their husbands were consumed by training at NASA, often travelling the country, their wives would wake up alone and go to bed alone. Many battled not only fear of the inherent dangers of their husband's jobs but loneliness too, and they leaned on each other for support. For some, drink and prescription drugs became a solution.

For the men, the Space Coast of Florida became their second home. Fourteen miles south of Kennedy Space Center is Cocoa Beach, an area which came alive during the space race as a popular astronaut hangout. As I type, I am sitting in the courtyard of a hotel that the Mercury Seven once owned here. In the lobby, a portrait of the seven men in their silvery spacesuits takes up one of the main walls. And outside, under a palm tree, a plaque pays homage to the hotel's former owners. Now returned to its former glory, the accommodation is set over two floors, centred around a pool and a small running track.

During the space race, this hotel was the scene of notorious astronaut parties and a place where many would entertain other women. While astronauts were portrayed as the perfect family men, their extra-marital affairs were kept out of the public narrative – adulterer didn't quite have the same ring as 'all-American hero'. Though the wives often knew what was going on, staying married was almost a patriotic requirement; what woman would want to invite the press attention of a divorce, as well as bear the responsibility for the potentially deadly distraction it could have on their husband? But in the years after the Moon landing, a lot of the marriages of NASA's first astronauts did end in divorce. Many grew tired of their lives being married to somebody else's hero.

Other women were left as widows raising children alone when their husbands were tragically killed during training. As the space programme was so new, there was little in the way of support for astronaut widows, and many chose to move away from the space communities in Houston's suburbs following tragedies. They were no longer the wives of an astronaut; the life they had – and the perks that came with it – would die with their husbands.

Martha Chaffee was just 27 when her husband Roger died in the Apollo 1 fire. She had to tell her five-year-old son and eight-year-old daughter that their father wasn't coming home. She also had to live with the knowledge that her husband died having never travelled to space – something they had both dedicated their lives to.

Before his death, Gus Grissom had told his wife Betty, 'If I die, have a party.' Betty never held that party. Instead, she sued the manufacturers of her late husband's spacecraft. Awarded $350,000 (the equivalent of $3 million today), she paved the way for other widows to do the same.

But, like Pat White and Martha Chaffee, the trauma of her husband's death stayed with her. Every year for the rest of her life, on the anniversary of the fire, Betty Grissom made the pilgrimage to the launch complex where her husband had lost his life.

A particularly grim story from this era is of Valentina Yakovlevna, wife of the Soviet cosmonaut Vladimir Komarov. In April 1967, Vladimir was launched into space in the Soyuz 1. He embarked on the mission knowing that the spacecraft had faults, making it extremely dangerous. Once in orbit, it quickly became apparent that Vladimir's failing spacecraft could not get him back to Earth alive. Valentina was left to say goodbye to her husband over the radio. Some time after that conversation, Vladimir began his final journey, which would see his spacecraft plummet to Earth without a functioning parachute.

In those early days of human spaceflight, nobody had planned what to do for those loved ones left on the ground should a space traveller discover they would not be making it home alive. Just as a lack of foresight had contributed to accidents, there was also a failure to consider the human impact when something went wrong.

Today, space travel remains hugely risky. For astronauts, the odds of not making it home alive have been said to stand at something like 1 in 62. Imagine going to work knowing the odds of you not making it home are 1 in 62? Even today, under NASA's Commercial Crew Programme, the requirement for a vehicle is 1 in 270. And while everything is done to ensure that nothing *will* go wrong, there are now plans in place to handle losses. For NASA, that means looking at all potential issues and planning for them, including how families will be supported during the mission and what would be needed should the worst happen. As we have learnt how to go to space, we have also had to learn how to deal with the 'on Earth' consequences of the risks involved.

*

As Apollo 11 lifted off on the morning of 16 July 1969, watched by their wives and families, there was just one woman in the firing room: JoAnn Morgan. Sitting at her console with shoulder-length light-brown hair, wearing a dark, short-sleeved top, JoAnn stood out from the sea of white men in shirts and ties that surrounded her. She was in many ways as much a pioneer as the three men sitting in their spacecraft atop the rocket. A quiet hero immersed in a man's world, her determination to work in the space industry helped pave the way for others to follow in her footsteps.

Her fascination with reaching beyond Earth had been fuelled in part by her family's move to Florida when she was a teenager. Living near what would become the Space Coast, JoAnn could see rockets being tested across the river from her high school. At the time – the mid-1950s – NASA didn't yet exist and the rockets were being tested on Cape Canaveral Air Force base, next to where the Kennedy Space Center now stands. Later, when the first US satellite launched in January 1958, JoAnn saw the benefits that could come from this new frontier, not only from exploring, but from using this new vantage point to conduct science. While NASA would be the preserve of men for many years to come, a passion for space was not.

After seeing a job advert for an internship with the Army Ballistic Missile Agency (a facility where America's first space rockets were developed), JoAnn applied. The wording in the advert stated that 'students' were wanted. It said nothing about gender – had the word 'boys' been used instead of 'student', JoAnn said she would not have considered the role. That internship, and a subsequent degree in mathematics, set JoAnn on a path that led to her becoming the first woman to work as an engineer at NASA's Kennedy Space Center.

Before her arrival, a meeting had been held, attended by every single person who would be working with her. They were told that there was a 'young lady joining, who wants to be an engineer' and that they should 'treat her like an engineer'. The response from one of the men in the room was, 'Can we ask her to make coffee?'

And so JoAnn's journey into the unknowns of being a woman at NASA in the 1960s began. It would be at times a voyage of loneliness – wherever she went, she was the only woman. Many of the buildings she worked in didn't even have toilets for women – NASA might have been developing the capabilities to send humans to the Moon, but on Earth they had still not developed the onsite facilities for a member of the opposite sex. Instead, when JoAnn needed to use the restroom, a security guard had to clear out the men and then stand guard. Imagine how humiliating that must have felt.

Though JoAnn was just as passionate about space and talented as the men around her, it was often made very hard for her to do her job. During her early career she experienced obscene phone calls and, at one systems test, she was physically hit over the back by a supervisor and told she had to leave. His reason was simply that he didn't allow women at the test site. But JoAnn kept going, later likening what she experienced to the mosquitos in the blistering heat of Florida: 'You swat them, then you're done with it and you keep going.'

By the summer of 1969, as NASA got ready to send humans to the surface of the Moon, JoAnn was now a senior engineer. Despite the sexism and discrimination from some, she had succeeded in working on all the US human spaceflight projects: Mercury, Gemini and now Apollo. Yet she was still not permitted in the firing room during lift-off. That was deemed a 'man's place', for no good reason. On the launch days of previous missions, over 200 engineers – many JoAnn's colleagues with whom she worked on a daily basis – had sat in the firing room, monitoring different systems and communicating any issues, before the launch director could give the final 'go' for lift-off. It's a powerful moment, to witness from this vantage point something you have worked on for years come to life and take humans away from Earth.

Despite the fact that her job as instrument controller for the launch of Apollo 11 needed to be done from the firing room, JoAnn's supervisor had to go to the top at NASA, seeking permission for her to be there – to simply do the job she was qualified to do required special permission. But that permission was granted and JoAnn finally took her place as the only woman in the firing room for the launch of Apollo 11.

As the roar of the Saturn V, bound for the Moon, ripped through the bright blue Florida sky, it represented not just a moment of reckoning for America, but also for JoAnn and the many women who would follow in her footsteps. In those moments she finally felt like she was part of the team, even though she had worked there for years.

In the coming decades, JoAnn would go on to become one of NASA's most successful engineers, and one of the most decorated women at the Kennedy Space Center. The girl who had grown up seeing some of the first rockets being tested retired having worked on our future – on rovers on the surface of Mars. Her passion for space never wavered. In her own words: 'The new knowledge we are going to get is so profound it is worth my life to work on it.'

When NASA celebrated the fiftieth anniversary of the launch of Apollo 11 with a gala dinner at the Kennedy Space Center, it was JoAnn who stood on stage. Honoured that night with the Pioneer Award, she credited her success to the motto that she lived by: be fearless, love what you do and follow your passion.

Today, the photograph of her sitting among a sea of men serves not only as inspiration, but as a poignant reminder of how we failed so many in our early pursuit of space. Equality in the space industry matters, because when we leave Earth, we are representing all of humanity. There are 7.6 billion humans on this planet. If we are to succeed in continuing to push the limits of what is possible, then space needs to continue to be inclusive. There are technical problems to solve that are beyond what we currently know how to do. We need creative people capable of the freshest, most original thinking. We can't afford to exclude anyone.

*

For others, the story of their contributions to both space exploration and equality would go by unnoticed by all but a few for decades. When Katherine Johnson died at the age of 101 in February 2020, her passing made headlines around the world. By this time, she was a global icon. A film, called *Hidden Figures*, which was adapted from a book of the same name, had been made about her life, and when she appeared on stage at the Oscars in 2017 she was greeted by a standing ovation. But back when Katherine worked for NASA, she was merely referred to as 'the girl with the numbers'.

Born in 1918, before humans had succeeded in crossing the Atlantic by aeroplane, Katherine not only grew up in an era of great change and progress, she helped to create history herself. Having excelled at maths as a child, Katherine became one of three African–American students who were the first to integrate into West Virginia's previously all-white graduate schools. After a spell teaching – and armed with an education still not available to many of her peers – she began her career at what was then the National Advisory Committee for Aeronautics (which would later become NASA) as one of the many women who worked as 'human computers' in its laboratory in Langley.

At this time, thanks to innovations in flight and rocketry, there were streams of data and calculations to perform that today we now rely on computers to do. Female mathematicians were used to process numbers, as it was cost-effective: more women were receiving a university maths education and were capable of the work, and they could be paid less than a man to do the same job.

The male engineers may have seen what the 'human computers' did as routine, but the reality was it required highly advanced mathematical skills. Working behind the scenes, spending days looking at streams of numbers and doing sometimes brain-bending calculations by hand, it was these women who made the work of the engineers possible. Without modern computers, everything they were trying to achieve in pushing the limits of flight – and later space – relied on the numbers being right.

Though low paying compared with the jobs taken by men, the 'human computers' earned better wages than they would have in most other roles available at the time. Also, unlike many professions, married women with children were allowed to work in these jobs. And, while most of the 'human computers' were white, African-American women could apply – at a time when there were really only two traditional professional roles open to black women in the USA: teaching and nursing.

But this was the Jim Crow era, and at work they still faced segregation: divided into different offices, eating in different canteens and using separate bathrooms – marked for 'whites' and 'coloureds'. The division inside the office was merely a reflection of the grim divisions of life outside, with the women returning home to separate communities and often contrasting fortunes.

By 1956, Katherine was a widow and a single mother, after her husband died of cancer. But despite this, and the adversity she faced as an African-American woman in a white man's world, she continued to excel at her work. In 1958, as NACA turned into NASA (and the organisation ceased to segregate its staff), the pressure was on for America to succeed in the space race. With this came an opportunity for Katherine to pave the way not only for African-Americans in the American space programme, but for humanity's successes in space. Katherine worked on calculations that had never been done before, such as predicting the trajectory of a spacecraft – essentially the path that a spacecraft follows in flight. Something you probably don't even think about when you think of space travel, but it is crucial to working out how we return astronauts safely to Earth. Through her work at NASA,

Katherine became a pioneer in the calculations behind spaceflights.

By the early 1960s, actual computers were beginning to replace the work of the 'human computers', yet the technology was relatively new and prone to technical problems and blackouts. The early astronauts often didn't trust the computers. Before climbing into his spacecraft to become the first American to orbit the Earth, astronaut John Glenn requested that Katherine manually check the computer's calculations. It's claimed that he said, 'If she says they're good, then I am good to go.' And so Katherine proceeded to check the computer's calculations by hand. This is something that is complex enough today even with all the advantages of modern computing.

Katherine went on to develop the calculations that helped humans successfully land on the Moon, quietly continuing to work at NASA on the mathematics behind spaceflight, defying the prejudices of the era that held back so many.

Appearing on stage at the Oscars at nearly 100 years old, Katherine was introduced to the crowd as an 'American hero'; some in the audience were left close to tears as she smiled and waved. She was also, in 2015, a recipient of the Presidential Medal of Freedom – America's highest civilian honour. But for more than half a century she was just one of the many quiet heroes of the Space Age, who did not seek praise and was not recognised for all she did, but who helped to give us the world that we so often take for granted today.

*

It took until the 1980s for who we were sending to space to begin to resemble who we are on Earth. By the time the crew of *Challenger* prepared for their ill-fated mission, slated for launch in early 1986, the type of people who were going into space had changed. While the first NASA astronauts had been from the military, now the requirements for the job were much broader. Astronauts were also scientists and physicians and – most importantly – they were no longer just white men.

Through the Space Shuttle programme, that would begin flying in 1981, for the first time NASA recruited astronauts of different ethnicities and actively sought to select women. Not only were cultures and attitudes changing, but so was the reason for going to space. The goal was for Earth orbit to become more easily accessible, and many missions were now focused on science – with more room on the shuttle for experiments than on previous spacecraft. And so the qualities needed to become an astronaut expanded. Of the 35 astronauts recruited at the end of the 1970s, six were women. Two decades after the Soviets had sent Valentina Tereshkova into orbit, Sally Ride became the first US woman to make the trip in June 1983. Two months after her, Guion Bluford became the first African-American and second person of African descent (the Soviet Union had once again pipped NASA to the post in 1980, sending the Cuban Arnaldo Tamayo Méndez, who was also of African descent).

By the mid-1980s, thanks to the shuttle and its capacity to carry up to seven crew (meaning not every astronaut had to be a pilot), it had been decided that a teacher was going to make the journey. Christa McAuliffe, a historian, social studies teacher and mother of two from Concord, New Hampshire, had been selected from over 11,000 people who had applied for the US government's Teacher in Space Project. The programme's aim was to help maintain American successes in space exploration. It was hoped that by sending Christa – a teacher, and a child of the Space Age, who had been inspired by seeing the flights of the Mercury Seven – on a space mission, she would go on to inspire children across the country. America needed to improve its education of science and maths, and the idea was that a teacher would not only make space more relatable to students, but also encourage other teachers and help to inject some much-needed enthusiasm into the job. So Christa would not become an astronaut but instead a spaceflight participant who would experience space for the benefit of educating others. She represented what she called 'the ordinary person'.

Along with her backup, teacher Barbara Morgan (astronaut crews always had backups, in case something should go wrong during training), Christa spent a year with NASA, training for the rigours of spaceflight. By this time, space travel was starting to become routine – at least to the public. Enthusiasm had stagnated and news of astronauts going to space was often relegated to a small section of the newspaper. In 1985, the year leading up to Christa's flight, launches of the shuttle had become almost monthly. But with the build-up to Christa's journey came renewed public excitement and talk of how space would soon be accessible to the masses and no longer just the preserve of professional (and highly trained) astronauts.

Christa's wide smile and infectious enthusiasm for both teaching and space exploration soon saw her become a new type of celebrity, with television crews and the public following her every step. She wanted to 'humanise the Space Age'. During her planned six days in orbit, Christa intended to broadcast live to school children, giving lessons and providing a guided tour of the inside of the spacecraft. The public related to Christa, and anticipation around the mission rivalled that of Apollo.

On the morning of 28 January 1986, Christa, along with commander Dick Scobee, pilot Michael J. Smith and astronauts Ellison Onizuka, Judy Resnik, Ron McNair and Greg Jarvis, followed in the tradition of breakfast in the astronaut crew quarters at Kennedy Space Center. Then, dressed in their blue flight suits, they waved to reporters as they walked out to the van which would take them to *Challenger*. There had been several delays to the launch, but there was confidence that today would be the day. As they boarded the spacecraft, a member of the closeout crew gave Christa an apple – a symbol of appreciation for the teacher in space.

Seventy-three seconds after lift-off, *Challenger* broke apart. The compartment that the crew were in remained intact as it tumbled for 2 minutes and 45 seconds over a distance of more than 8.5 miles before smashing into the ocean. All seven lost their lives. While it was likely the crew were alive for the fall, it is not known if they were conscious all this time, although some senior investigators believed that commander Dick Scobee did everything he could to fly the now-wingless craft in those horrifying last few minutes.

A matter of miles away at the Kennedy Space Center the crowds – including Christa McAuliffe's parents and children from her school – watched on helplessly as the sky filled with smoke and the ominous words 'there's obviously been a major malfunction' bellowed over the onsite speakers. For a long moment, few realised the true horror of what they had witnessed. Then screams, tears and confusion. School children across the country had stopped lessons to watch the launch; now they were witnessing the unthinkable. The haunting images of what to many looked like an explosion played on loop across the news channels. Christa's parents and family were taken to her room in the astronaut crew quarters, the trainers she had been wearing just a few hours earlier still lying by her bed.

In the coming months, the cause of the disaster was found to be the failure of one of the O-ring seals – essentially rubber rings designed to seal the joints on the solid rocket boosters on the side of the shuttle. Because of the unusually cold weather, the rubber in one of the O-rings had become stiff, thus failing to seal the joint.

During launch, hot gases bathed the external tank of the Space Shuttle, causing it to rupture. At 73 seconds, the forces became too great and it tore the Space Shuttle apart. Some engineers had warned about the possibility of the O-ring failing, but there was pressure to not delay the launch.

For all the great things we have achieved in exploring space, there have been horrifying failures, and *Challenger* was the most terrible to date, not least because Christa's presence had in some ways given the false impression to the public that space travel was 'safe' and 'routine'. The *Challenger* disaster haunted the space programme, and not just because many believe it could have been avoided. For the first time in US history, a spacecraft had been lost during flight and the awful moment had been filmed for the world to see. During subsequent launches, those watching on would always give a sigh of relief once lift-off had passed the fateful 73-second mark. It would take nearly three years for a shuttle to fly again, and missions were never as frequent as before the disaster. Going to space was no longer seen as easy, or routine.

Almost 17 years to the day after the loss of *Challenger* came another tragedy for NASA when Space Shuttle *Columbia* failed to return to Earth. Its destruction during re-entry again cost the lives of the seven astronauts on board – among them Kalpana Chawla, the first Indian woman to travel to space. The cause of the accident was missing heat shield tiles on the leading edge of the orbiter's wings, which had been lost during take-off.

The combination of these two disasters meant that the shuttle could no longer be considered the low-cost reusable space vehicle it was designed to be; instead it had become a complex and costly machine that had now taken 14 lives.

However, to date, more people have travelled to space on the shuttle than on any other spacecraft. It launched (and then later repaired) the Hubble Space Telescope – as well as being used to conduct a huge amount of science in space to benefit life on Earth. And it was instrumental in the construction of the International Space Station.

Even having lost colleagues and friends, astronauts were still prepared to return to flight. To keep exploring. To keep pushing the limits of what was possible. Among those who went to space after these disasters was Barbara Morgan, Christa's backup, who, in 2007, orbited the Earth, completing Christa's dream. In many ways, the sacrifice of those who lost their lives acts not as a deterrent, but instead calls loudly to others to fulfil their promise. As with any new frontier, lives will be lost, but to stop exploring because of risk would be a greater sorrow. Instead, we continue in their name.

In her lessons, Christa McAuliffe would tell her students stories not just of well-known figures from history, but tales of the 'ordinary people', using letters and diaries. She also asked her students to complete oral history projects, interviewing elderly members of the community. She explained that, 'It is easy to chronical military, political and economic history, but the common man was often pushed aside.'

In addition to her science lessons from space, she was planning to keep a diary. In an era long before social media, her diary would have been the first record of the experience of space travel from someone who wasn't an astronaut. Christa wanted to show her students that the little person counts, that anyone can have an effect on our society and the world. That the ordinary person contributes to history too.

Although she never got to complete her mission, her quest to inspire future generations lives on. In the aftermath of her death, specialist space education facilities – known as 'Challenger Learning Centers' – were set up across the world. Here, children continue to be inspired by space and the idea that the sky is no longer the limit. Although I was just a baby when the *Challenger* accident happened, I am among those who benefited from these centres, attending one as a teenager. An ordinary person who did an extraordinary thing, Christa McAuliffe is remembered not for the manner in which she died, but for how she lived her life.

More than anything, space gives us heroes. Not just the famous pioneers whose names are publicly recorded – there are many of whom you may not have heard, but who have quietly pursued the extraordinary. Their dedication and determination can serve as inspiration for all of us. Perhaps this is one of the greatest things to come from space exploration: it's not just about the knowledge gained, but the stories of these many unsung heroes and of the great things we can achieve through curiosity, imagination and hard work. That so many dedicate their lives to the pursuit of exploring beyond Earth despite the risks illustrates the value of what they are chasing – being part of leaving our planet and opening up the possibilities of space. In many ways, it is not our successes but our failures and how we respond to them that define us, along with the resilience and determination to keep exploring even in the face of the known dangers.

Although it was the uneasy chill of the Cold War that first pushed us into space, what we have done since is about science and extending the capabilities of where we as humans can exist. Going to space is a triumph for our ingenuity, but it is also a story of the human condition, of the greatness that we can achieve when we work together, the sacrifices that some are willing to make for a higher calling and how ordinary people can achieve the extraordinary.

As I look again at the portraits of fallen astronauts in the Astronauts Memorial Foundation offices, the faces no longer seem like those of the grown-ups who inspired me as a child. They are mostly in their thirties and forties, and now look more like my peers. While I have been lucky enough to age, they have not. As we continue to look up and push forward in space exploration, they will remain forever young – just as those who have given their lives in the pursuit of great and good things on Earth. The number of faces on that wall will sadly grow, but so will the value of what they gave their lives for. Space is our future, and we would do those who have come before us a disservice if we do not continue to explore.

Chapter Three

SPACE ON EARTH

'Man must rise above the Earth – to the
top of the atmosphere and beyond – for
only thus will he fully understand the world
in which he lives.'

Socrates

B etween 1968 and 1971, the now-defunct airline Pan Am
began printing membership cards for its 'First Moon
Flights' Club. Customers could put their names down on
a list for the first tourist trips to the Moon. Of course, it
was primarily a marketing stunt – Pan Am didn't actually
have a vehicle capable of making the trip – but this was
a time during which humans had begun walking on the
Moon. Space was prominent in the public consciousness.
The possibility of booking a ticket to go yourself felt
tantalisingly close.

The idea of the club is said to have come from an
Austrian journalist called Gerhard Pistor who, in 1964,
during the height of the space race, went to a travel agency
in an attempt to book a flight to the Moon. The request
was forwarded to Pan Am who, two weeks later, accepted
it, claiming that they expected their lunar flights to the
Moon to start in the year 2000.

Excitement about the airline's potential to one day travel
to space was later fuelled by a cameo in the 1968 movie
2001: A Space Odyssey, which showed Pan Am ferry-
ing passengers across space, complete with a stewardess
gingerly walking in the microgravity environment, thanks
to some special grip footwear.

In total, more than 90,000 people signed up for the First Moon Flights Club. In return, they received a numbered card, signed by the airline's vice president of sales and featuring a drawing of two future lunar tourists on the surface of the Moon, with the Earth in the background.

With those first few trips to space had come a 'space fever', and it touched nearly every aspect of our culture of the time. *Vogue* even ran features on space fashion as designers clambered to dress people for what they assumed would be the next frontier. There were space-themed toys and TV shows; *The Jetsons* and *Fireball XL5* both first appeared in 1962 shortly after humans had started travelling to space. Even food took on a Space Age look, and adverts offered everything from 'Space Age tailoring' to 'Space Age refrigerators' and cleaning products, because 'women of the future will make the Moon a cleaner place'.

For those who lived through this time it was perhaps almost impossible not to be inspired by space and the promise of what was to come from leaving Earth. Many just assumed that the coming decades would see more and more people making the journey into space. And it wasn't just the science-fiction writers or the marketing men who were filling our heads with dreams of space. Scientists, engineers and visionaries – some of the very brightest and best minds of the time – were taking the possibility of extending human presence into space pretty seriously too. In upstate New York, not far from Niagara Falls, one company had even started building jetpacks.

Perhaps the epitome of Space Age technology, the jetpack

made its first flight the same month that Yuri Gagarin became the first person to travel into space. Engineers at Bell Aerospace who worked on it would continue to develop all kinds of seemingly crazy contraptions – such as flying chairs and flying pogo sticks – the idea being that future space explorers could use them on other worlds. While these might seem a bit ludicrous from the perspective of today, they were all part of the bold vision for space future in the 1960s, to help not only send people to the Moon, but eventually further into space.

Bell Aerospace also designed what can only be described as a 'flying bedstead', and it was nicknamed accordingly. More formally known as the LLTV (Lunar Landing Training Vehicle), the four-legged contraption consisted of a metallic frame with a seat at the front and was used by some of the first astronauts to simulate what it would be like to land on the Moon. A downward-pointing turbofan on the LLTV counteracted much of the vehicle's weight, helping to give the astronauts a sense of what it would be like to pilot it in the Moon's gravity.

So compared with the flying bedstead, all these other crazy contraptions didn't seem too implausible. Bell Aerospace even hoped its flying pogo sticks would be used by Apollo astronauts on the Moon, but the company lost out to the lunar rover.

In Queens, New York, the 1964 World's Fair vividly brought alive our dreams for a future in space, as companies showcased their visions for our today. The General Motors Futurama 2 ride guided passengers on a voyage into our future, complete with Moon bases, robotic lunar rovers crawling across the lunar surface and astronauts in space monitoring Earth. The fair even included a NASA-sponsored rocket park, giving the public a chance to get close to the giants that had taken us on our story with the stars thus far.

We have to appreciate the staggering rate of acceleration in technology at this point. The timespan between the first person going into space and humans walking on the surface of the Moon was little more than eight years. In this period, space travel evolved from something that was barely possible to the point where people could land a spacecraft on the Moon. So the idea that you yourself could soon follow in these footsteps – or at the very least your children – wasn't too farfetched.

At NASA, staff began looking very seriously at the feasibility of sending humans to the planet Mars. In 1969, a month after the Apollo 11 Moon landings, Wernher von Braun presented to the Space Task Group plans to land humans on the Martian surface by 1982. This group had been commissioned by President Nixon to assess what could be done post-Apollo. Von Braun stated that, after the Moon landing, the next frontier would be human exploration of the planets, in pursuit of an answer to what he called 'the most significant scientific question' – the possibility of extra-terrestrial life elsewhere in our solar system.

His paper showcased plans to assemble a vehicle in Earth's orbit to help reduce the weight of launch, which would then be used to take astronauts to Mars. While von

Braun acknowledged that it would be a 'great undertaking', he reasoned the challenge would be no greater than that set in 1961 to 'land a man on the Moon'. After the success of the lunar landings, it seemed like the next logical step.

The plans for the mission showed three astronauts on the surface of Mars spending 30–60 days on the planet before returning to Earth. This wasn't fantasy; the potential was there. Von Braun's design even allowed for the possibility of creating gravity for the Mars-bound astronauts by attaching two spacecraft together and rotating them. Some may wonder where we could have been by now if we had landed on Mars in the 1980s. But, of course, much to the frustration of many from this era, and to those who dedicated their lives to spaceflight, it didn't happen. More than five decades after the first Moon landing, Mars seems as far away today as it did then.

So what went wrong? The main reason for a slowing down of our space dreams was to do with both politics and money. The Moonshot, while satisfying our innate curiosity to explore, was about two superpowers racing to do a big thing well. Once America had landed on the Moon, there was little political reason to continue. The nation had won, and while many dreamed of continuing to the stars, plenty of taxpayers had grown frustrated with the huge sums of money being spent racing to this seemingly 'dull, lifeless rock' when there were so many other problems facing life on Earth.

President Nixon was presented with the options of

a Mars landing by the early 1980s alongside plans for a lunar base and a space station accommodating tens of people, but none of it happened. It was hard to justify the cost of space exploration. In reality, at the height of the space race in 1965, spending on NASA from the federal budget was just 4 per cent, reducing to less than 1 per cent from the 1970s, but still Americans were divided about whether the cost of the Moon landings had been worth it.

In December 1972, Apollo 17 became the last mission to the surface of the Moon. The mission's commander, Gene Cernan, would die in 2017 still holding the title of 'last person on the Moon'. In total, just 12 human beings walked on the lunar surface during the Apollo era. The jetpack was consigned to movies and stunts at public events and the First Moon Flight Club membership cards ended up in museums and attics. Parts of the 1964 World's Fair can still be seen in Flushing Meadows, New York, with the NASA rockets standing among trees with the Manhattan skyline in the background, stranded relics of our Space Age dreams.

*

The great promises of the Space Age slowly slipped away in the decades following the final Apollo Moon landing, but this didn't mean we stopped going to space. Instead, what opened up were possibilities that many had not thought of, but that have profoundly changed the way we live. So many of our predictions for space exploration had been about people leaving the planet that we almost failed to see how space would instead become about Earth. This essentially happened in two ways: we began to develop technology invented for space so we could use it on Earth, and we learnt how to use the platform that a presence in space gives us to improve life on our planet.

So what springs to mind when I ask, 'What technologies has space given us?' I'm sure for a number of us it's Velcro and Teflon pans. It's a common misconception that NASA invented these two things for space travel. In fact, both were invented beforehand, NASA just made them famous, using Velcro so that astronauts could stop things floating away by 'sticking' it to the inside of their spacecraft, and Teflon for spacesuits and heat shields.

There are, however, many surprising items that owe their beginnings to space. Let's start with your bedroom. Look at your bed. Perhaps you are lucky enough to own a memory foam mattress? Memory foam was developed by NASA when they were looking for ways to cushion test pilots during flights. Do you ever clean your house with a cordless, handheld 'Dust Buster' vacuum? These too started their life being developed for space – during a collaboration between NASA and the company Black & Decker to build battery-operated tools for lunar exploration. Elsewhere in your house, you hopefully have at least one fire alarm. Should the worst happen and a fire breaks out, the firefighters who come to your assistance will be wearing clothing made of flame-resistant materials which were first developed for spacesuits. The portable breathing apparatus they may need to wear also owes its conception to space – it was originally developed for astronauts who needed breathing systems that were as light and compact as possible to take into space.

Perhaps you are into sport – you or someone you know may have run a marathon or a half marathon. Those thin, silver metallic blankets that are sometimes given out to runners who have just finished a long race to keep them warm, or are found in emergency survival packs, look pretty spacey and they do indeed link back to space. The technology for the material of these insulating blankets comes from NASA and can be found on the Hubble Space Telescope and Mars rovers, helping to maintain the temperature of equipment in the extremes of space.

If running isn't your thing, what about winter sports? If you ski or snowboard, perhaps the goggles you wear have scratch-resistant sun-filtering lenses. This technology was first developed by NASA for astronaut helmet visors.

Even modern aeroplane travel is connected to space. Pilots today use digital flight controls, which owe their beginnings to the Space Age. Before the Moon landings, pilots controlled planes mechanically; the computer guidance and controls that we have now were developed for NASA to help guide the astronauts to the lunar surface. The system used by the commercial plane you travel on to take a holiday is a descendant of the one that helped pilot humans to the surface of another world.

Off the west coast of Australia, technology originally developed by NASA for spacecraft is being used to help researchers track whale sharks and understand more about their migration patterns. Like the early explorers who crossed our seas, spacecraft also use the stars to assist with navigation. Onboard star-trackers observe slices of the sky and take photographs, which are then compared to star maps on the spacecraft's computer so that it knows where it is. Whale sharks have distinct sets of markings above their gills and on their fins – effectively their own sets of fingerprints – which are as unique as star patterns in the sky. Using photographs taken by both tourists and professionals, researchers can use the same techniques as the NASA star-trackers to compare the patterns of spots to an existing database and understand more about the migration of these creatures. We are learning more about the great unknowns of our oceans thanks to our exploration of the great unknowns of space.

Today, there are literally thousands of applications of technologies that owe their origins to space travel. NASA alone creates 1,600 new technologies every year, from materials to software and robotics. At NASA's Johnson Space Center, I have watched engineers work on new concepts for robotic exoskeletons, worn like a metallic suit over the legs and waist and looking like something straight out of the *Iron Man* movies. The idea is to provide astronauts with increased strength when exploring other planets in the future. But this type of technology also has the potential to provide hope to many on Earth with mobility problems, even helping people who have lost the use of their legs to be able to walk again. So much of what we do in space has more uses beyond simply 'leaving Earth'.

Of course, it is likely that some of these ideas would have come about had we not gone into space, but our ambitions in space exploration have accelerated the development of technology, as they have forced us to come up with ways of doing things we have never done before.

However, our space age of today is more than spin-offs from technology developed for space exploration. So much of what we do in our everyday lives relies on satellites in space. You may think about the space industry as something that is focused outwards into the universe, that's about exploring and pushing the limits of human endeavours, and while this is true, the reality is that most of what we do is concerned with looking back at Earth. Our twenty-first-century space age is what I like to call the 'unexpected space age', and it's about all of us.

Right now, there are thousands of operating satellites orbiting above us and the number is growing all the time. You may occasionally see one passing by, looking like a 'moving star' in our night sky. When we look up at the heavens, we do not just see the same sky that our ancestors saw, we occasionally see what we have added, as we have gone to space and figured out how to use this vantage point to benefit ourselves.

Satellites give us a 'bird's-eye view' of our planet, so to speak, allowing large areas of the Earth to be observed at a time, gathering data more quickly than we could on the ground. They also enable us to communicate with ease across the globe, with signals sent into space and redirected to elsewhere on the planet.

Owned by both governments and private companies, and powered either by batteries or solar panels, these satellites use onboard antennas to send and receive information. Often they have sensors to make observations. They can even communicate with each other and can be strategically placed to provide complete global coverage. Their uses include navigation, forecasting the weather, protecting borders, fighting terrorism, aiding peacekeeping missions that rely on secure communications, and monitoring deforestation, to name but a few. Even the food you eat has benefited from technology in space, as farmers are able to access satellite images of their crops to help better monitor everything from their rate of growth to how moist the land is.

If you look around, you will find that our space age of today is closer than you realise. It may even be next to you. And if not, it is certainly not far away. It is the one device you most likely cannot live without … it is your smartphone.

From checking in with your location on social media, to ordering take-away food, calling a car to take you somewhere or using a map to get directions, your phone is constantly receiving signals from satellites to calculate your position, based upon the location of the satellite and your distance from it. Though it might not seem like it, your smartphone is your own personal space receiver, a device that connects all of us to space.

While a generation was dreaming of jetpacks, they never imagined Deliveroo. Even though we've been launching satellites since the late 1950s, no one during the heyday of the space race predicted a future of cyberspace – the internet that we have become so reliant on. But the combination of the connected world we live in today and the satellites above us is what has fuelled the unexpected space age. We can even use apps on our personal space receiver to look up and explore the night sky or watch live images of rocket launches elsewhere on the planet.

We have reached a point where there is often a blurring of the lines as to what is a tech company and what is a space company. For example, if you use an app on your phone to order a cab to come and pick you up, is this a tech company because you are using an app? Or a space company, because the app relies on satellites in space to find your position and then map how to get to your destination? The answer is both, though many of us probably don't think about the space element.

But it isn't just smartphone apps that benefit from satellites. If we buy something – say a coffee – on a credit or debit card or withdraw cash from an ATM, satellites are used here too. These transactions need to be timed to the nanosecond – banks rely on time stamps to monitor transactions and detect fraud. GPS – Global Positioning System – the same technology that puts a map on your phone, is also used for precision timings, sending the exact same time to everywhere on the planet. Our whole modern world of finance is reliant on space-based technology. It is in the weather forecast we check. It is in the precise train and bus times that can be tracked. It is in 'share my location' and 'find my phone'. It is in the ability to pull out your phone, look up at the night sky and know what we are looking at, no matter where you are in the world. This combination of satellites in space and modern technology enabled by the internet is everywhere.

We make use of our connections in space nearly every minute of our waking lives. Even our electricity grid relies on satellites for precision timing – so every time you put on the kettle or turn on the lights, you are using space technology. And of course those lights and that kettle can be turned on using just your voice, thanks to internet smart home devices.

It might not look like the future that was imagined back in the 1960s when we dreamed of holidays in space and people visited the rockets at the World's Fair, but even so, the technological advances in our world of today are only possible because of space exploration. Just imagine a day without space. Without satellites, so much of the technology we rely on would not work. This is our unexpected space age. And it makes our lives so much easier that we don't even think about it.

*

While much of the technology we've become used to today is about making our relatively affluent lives in the West more convenient, how is it benefiting those who are the poorest and most vulnerable elsewhere on the planet? If we are to succeed in continuing to use and explore space, more and more people need to receive the benefits that can come from the combination of satellite and internet technology.

If you were to take a map of the world and colour in the countries that have access to their own satellites, you would colour around three-quarters of the land mass on Earth, and that's growing all the time. As satellites have become smaller and require fewer people to operate them from the ground, more and more countries have been able to join the space age, helping to bridge the gap between the haves and the have-nots. Essentially, satellites are an investment that helps developing countries to grow their economies and improve the quality of life for their people.

Satellites are able to efficiently monitor reservoir levels, providing early warnings of water shortages. They can image farmland, providing information to help with crop yield and productivity. And they can help monitor borders, improving security. There are now so many ways in which space technology is improving lives and offering hope to people across the planet. Let's have a look at few key areas.

The first is that satellites can provide the internet from space, which can make a huge difference in places where it's not possible to get the internet any other way. Whereas your internet very likely comes from wireless cell towers or cables routed into homes and offices, internet from space works by beaming the signals from satellites to a terminal on the ground which is connected to a computer, making it possible to get online.

In the future, this offers the potential to bridge the digital divide. Across the world, there are currently around four billion people who do not have access to the internet. In Africa, for example, roughly half the population have mobile phones, but only a quarter can get online. So many people are missing out on the opportunities that come from being able to access the internet: education, banking, business and new ideas. Instead of having to put in infrastructure on the ground, something that would be a huge challenge, providing the internet from satellites offers a potential solution to connecting many more people across the world and giving them access to so much of the things all of us in the West rely on every day, often without thinking about it.

In rural areas of Nigeria, for example, inadequate infrastructure, a lack of basic services and not enough skilled medical workers have led to low standards of healthcare for many. Fifty-eight thousand women die in childbirth every year, the country has the third-highest infant mortality rate in the world and controlling the spread of infectious diseases presents a huge challenge.

There are some areas in Nigeria that are so remote they don't have access to the internet. But this connection is vital for improving healthcare in developing nations as it allows access to information, online medical training and advice from experts elsewhere in the world, quickly. As part of a project developed between health organisations in Nigeria, the UK Space Agency and a British satellite company called Inmarsat, some of these rural communities are being provided with connectivity from satellites in space.

What this has meant is that these remote clinics are no longer as isolated. Health workers can not only access support instantly, but also training videos and education so they are better able to respond to medical emergencies as they arise. It has also meant local governments can more easily capture information about diseases, making it possible to respond to potential outbreaks more quickly.

Another important field in which satellites are providing invaluable help is disaster relief. Even the poorest of places on Earth, countries that don't yet have access to their own satellites, are still able to use information from space to help the people on the ground. During the horrifying 2010 earthquake in Haiti – which hit the county's capital and left thousands of casualties – satellites assisted rescue workers as they dealt with the aftermath of the disaster.

As a result of the devastation, existing maps became out of date as so many roads were unpassable, but observations from space could provide real-time information about what was happening. Satellites gathered both optical and radar images – radar being particularly useful as it can 'see' through the clouds and also image at night – enabling rescue workers to get a picture of the full extent of the damage and figure out how best to gain access to areas that had been cut off and may have been most in need of help. Radar images were also able to identify hazards such as landslides, which can be triggered by earthquakes and could have put rescue workers or communities in further danger.

While money, politics, infrastructure and other Earth-based things of course play a part in our responses to disasters, the information we can gather from the perspective of space means that when we work to contain a terrible situation – fires, drought, deforestation, flooding – we do so far more effectively.

The benefits that space technology can bring to the world are not just about people; satellites help us monitor wildlife and protect some of the most vulnerable species on our planet. In sub-Saharan Africa, animals such as rhinos and elephants face an ongoing threat from poachers which is today at epidemic levels. Tackling the poaching problem is complex and expensive. These animals live on huge areas of land, making their movements difficult to monitor at ground level and poachers difficult to catch. However, even here in remote areas of our planet, anti-poaching units can use technology in space to try to protect these animals. Satellites can use radar with such precision that they are able to detect patterns of the movement of the animals on the ground. When this is combined with Earth-based information, conservation workers know more accurately the location of the animals they are trying to protect.

There is even the potential to use information from space to look for signs of unusual human activity, such as fires, which could have been started by potential poachers. Images are sent instantly to park rangers, who are able to access them thanks to the internet, meaning they can respond to situations in real time. This is something that is already working to save animals and lock up poachers. Thanks to a combination of human-made 'stars' silently orbiting our planet and the internet you and I use every single day, we are working to make the world a better place.

*

If you are lucky enough, on a clear night you can sometimes see the biggest human-made satellite, the International Space Station, passing overhead. Brighter than the brightest star, it takes a few minutes to completely traverse the night sky – appearing to us on Earth as a bright, single point of light. On board are normally six people, living and working in orbit – the thought that there is a human being looking down at our world from that bright light that passes overhead is a pretty powerful one.

In August 2018, two Russian cosmonauts opened the airlock of the International Space Station and stepped out into the void of space. Spacewalking, although necessary to maintain and install new components, is complex and of course carries risks – everything from decompression sickness to exhaustion to punctures in spacesuits which could potentially be fatal. It is something that requires many months of training and dedication, in order to get it right. The cosmonauts' mission that day was to install a new antenna, imaginatively called the International Cooperation for Animal Research Using Space, or ICARUS for short.

ICARUS is designed to help us understand more about all the other species with which we share the planet. And not just out of curiosity – what's happening to our wildlife acts as a warning system for the impact that humans are having on our environment. Scanning the Earth's surface from orbit, ICARUS can monitor hundreds of thousands of animals – which have been tagged with small sensors – and then transmit information such as their location, vital functions and activity back to scientists who are working to build up a global picture of animal behaviour. The goal: to decode the global interplay of life as part of the bigger picture in understanding our home.

In our modern, unexpected space age, space technology is enabling us to do so much more than explore. It is providing us with a new way of looking at our problems and understanding the world around us. However, it's not all about looking back and monitoring ourselves and our world. The International Space Station is, essentially, a giant orbiting scientific laboratory – albeit an expensive one. In fact, it is the most expensive human-made object ever created – at a cost of $150 billion. Much of the crew's time is dedicated to using the unique environment they are in – microgravity – to conduct scientific research to not only understand how humans can adapt to survive in space, but to learn more about how everything from materials to cells behave.

However, it is a common misconception that there is no gravity in space. At the distance the space station is from Earth, it still experiences around 90 per cent of the gravity from our planet, but because the space station is travelling so fast around the Earth, it is essentially in constant freefall, which is why everything onboard seems to 'float'. The term microgravity – used to describe this – is a rather confusing name as there is still gravity. In fact, everywhere you travel in space, you are essentially 'falling' towards larger objects, such as planets and moons, which is why it appears that astronauts are floating no matter where they travel.

When we first went into space, missions lasted just a matter of days – even the trips to the Moon were little more than a week long. But now space exploration is about longer trips, with crews spending months at a time aboard the space station. The reason behind this is that if we want to go further into space, we need to learn how to adapt to survive in microgravity. One of the biggest hurdles to humans exploring space is ourselves, our physiology, which was not meant for space travel. So among the research being conducted on the space station are experiments to understand what being in microgravity does to the human body. Effectively, astronauts are human guinea pigs, studying their own bodies, so that we can work out how they change in space and how we can learn to adapt to these changes. And this learning is not just important in space; it also teaches us things that benefit human life on Earth.

Astronauts who spend a long time in space are faced with weakening bones – the phrase 'use it or lose it' is as true in space as it is on Earth. During spaceflight, bone density decreases, as the bones no longer have to support the body against gravity as they do on Earth. The longer the period spent in space, the worse this problem is. If you have ever seen films of astronauts who have returned to Earth after a long time in space, you will notice that they have to be helped to walk. Essentially, they develop an accelerated version of osteoporosis coupled with weakened muscles, which they recover from when they return.

This is a huge hurdle for space exploration. If we want to go further into space, trips are going to last longer, which means that unless we are prepared to develop a way to simulate Earth's gravity, we need to find another method to prevent the weakening of astronauts' bones. At present, the best solution is to exercise for hours a day while in space, to try to combat some of the harmful effects not only on bones but also on muscles.

But learning how to deal with this accelerated version of osteoporosis is bringing real benefit to those who suffer from the disease here on Earth. As a direct result we now have new ways of diagnosing osteoporosis on Earth, a better understanding of the effects of diet and exercise, and new ways of testing medication.

And it is not just the bones or the muscles; microgravity

affects much of the body. There are changes to the immune system and cardiovascular issues, such as stiffening of the arteries – issues we often associate with ageing. Gathering data on what is happening in space is giving doctors the opportunity to study how we age and the potential to gather new insights as to how we might combat age-related diseases.

We know that, in microgravity, the human heart changes shape and becomes more spherical, while fluids in the body move towards the head, which means astronauts in space have increased pressure in their skulls. MRI scans have shown that, during long stays in space, the human brain shifts upwards in the skull. Some, but not all, astronauts even experience vision problems, which could be caused by the shifted brain pulling on the optic nerve. But we don't know why not everyone experiences this. There are still so many questions about how our bodies react away from Earth.

By studying these changes, and ways to potentially combat them for long-duration missions, scientists are having to find new solutions to problems caused by human spaceflight, which could again bring benefits to others suffering medical issues. For example, understanding pressure changes to the head in space and better ways to deal with this could potentially help with treating swelling caused by traumatic head injuries to patients on Earth.

In space, cells behave differently; their shape changes, the way they grow changes. In the absence (for all intents and purposes) of gravity, you are essentially able to look at things in a new way, to study behaviours which are normally masked by responses to gravity on Earth. This type of research into cells in the labs on the ISS is helping in the fight against cancer. It provides a new way of looking at how cells work and how – in the case of cancer – they can malfunction.

When medical research is conducted into cancer cells on Earth, due to gravity the cells grow in flat layers on dishes – think of this as comparable to looking like a stack of pancakes. But this doesn't actually fully simulate how they would behave in real life – in the body, cancer structures are 3D and almost spherical. By growing cancer cells in the microgravity environment of space, they arrange themselves into structures which more closely resemble how they would behave in the body. This is vital for researchers who are trying to pinpoint the cellular changes that cause cancer and has helped show how cancer cells would react to drugs differently. This understanding has also led to devices being created for cell research on Earth that replicate the effects of microgravity through rotating cells – a new way of doing medical research on Earth, thanks to space.

Of course, this research is not without risk. On 1 February 2003, the world watched in horror as the Space Shuttle *Columbia* disintegrated as it returned to Earth. From a height of 40 miles up, trails of smoke could be seen from the distant fireballs as they streaked across the blue cloudless sky, scattering the remains of *Columbia* and her crew of seven astronauts over three US states – Louisiana, Texas and Arkansas.

It was a heartbreaking tragedy, but the legacy of these astronauts lives on, not only through the many memorials across the world, but through the science that they had been doing in orbit as part of their mission.

As part of their work, during their 16 days in space, the crew was conducting round-the-clock research into new ways of attacking cancer cells. When *Columbia* disintegrated, it was assumed that the results of this work had been lost along with the crew. But the container with this and other experiments survived and was found during recovery efforts. Not only that, but many of the samples were in good condition – which allowed scientists to use the data collected by the astronauts to continue their research into treatments for cancer.

*

Of all of the benefits that exploring space has given us, arguably the greatest relates to one of the most important and pressing issues we face today: our planet's changing climate. We know the global temperature is rising, the oceans are warming, the ice sheets are shrinking, glaciers are retreating and there is a decrease of snow cover.

As we've seen, space-based technology provides us with an overview that we would not have been able to gather from the ground, enabling scientists to see the bigger picture. Satellites in orbit have helped give us the information needed to understand these changes and the impact of human activity. Much of the work that NASA and other space agencies do is to use the vantage point of Earth orbit to study our changing climate. Over many years, scientists have collected huge amounts of data about our planet and our climate on a global scale. Observations made by satellites have been used to help identify the impact of fossil fuels, produce the first global maps of carbon dioxide concentrations and show that both our ocean levels and temperatures are rising. Humans in space have also contributed to our understanding of our changing planet – astronauts on the International Space Station are able to observe and image extreme weather events on Earth.

The more information we have about what is going on, the better, and by combining this information from space with measurements gathered on the ground, climate scientists are able to use powerful computers to accurately model how our climate will continue to change. The more accurate data we have, the better we can predict the impact this will have on our future – a vital step in learning how to combat the problems we face.

By continuing to monitor Earth from space, not only can we work to better model what our climate future will look like, but also to develop ways of dealing with some of the now unavoidable changes, issues such as food and water security and an increase in the likelihood of unforeseen disastrous weather events. Sadly, the greatest negative effect will be felt by those who are the poorest on our planet, and human-made climate change also has the potential to be devastating not only to our species, but to the many other species with which we share our home.

Data gathered by satellites allow us to make more accurate predictions as to when extreme weather will happen. This means that we can provide people on the ground with better warning systems and as much information as possible so that they can prepare. We can also better monitor droughts, floods and harvests, and continue to gain an overview of the impact that our actions are having. Most importantly, the information we gather from space can help to shape policy about how we change our destructive actions.

While the 1960s saw some of the brightest minds in the world tackle the challenge of sending people to the Moon and returning them safely to Earth, our twenty-first-century Moonshot is about utilising space-based technology to look after our planet. Perhaps our next 'Apollo moment' will be if we can take all of the knowledge we are gathering from space and find a solution to the problem of our changing climate.

Climate scientists are working to give us as clear a picture as possible as to how our planet is changing and what the consequences will be. What they can't do is make us care, or make us act. It is down to all of us – you, me, industrialists, large corporations and policy makers – to use this information to make better decisions for our future. We need that same Apollo momentum –a world united in the pursuit of something greater. If space was able to do that for us once, it could do it again.

*

When the crew of Apollo 8 became the first humans to travel around the Moon in 1968 they carried with them two Hasselblad EL cameras, each with two lenses and seven magazines of 70mm film. As the astronauts orbited the Moon, they would be able to take pictures of the lunar surface as they scouted for potential landing sites. There was nothing in their flight plan – a minute-by-minute technical plan of the entire mission produced by NASA – about photographing the Earth above the surface of the Moon. Then, by chance, on their fourth orbit, the spacecraft was re-orientated and in the window appeared a view of half of Earth, our home, illuminated by the Sun, rising over the surface of the Moon. The crew had just become the first humans to ever see our planet in this way. A brilliant blue world floating in the nothingness of space.

Up until this point, the furthest that humans had travelled from Earth was about 850 miles. If you were to take a classroom globe and look at it, those first space explorers would be just a centimetre or so above the surface. From that perspective, although you can see the curvature of the Earth contrasting with the darkness of space, you cannot get a complete sense of just how small we really are. You need to be at least 20,000 miles away to see the Earth as a full globe; Apollo 8 reached 234,474 miles from Earth. Lunar probes had sent back grainy images of our planet, but nothing could have prepared Frank Borman, Jim Lovell and Bill Anders to be the first humans to see this view with their own eyes. There was a scramble to get the camera and photograph it.

That photo became known as *Earthrise*. The image of our partial Earth – a blue marble – rising over the surface of the Moon, is one of the most iconic images ever taken. In many ways it is our planet's first self-portrait – and it changed the way we viewed ourselves forever. This was the first time we truly saw our planet from afar. For the entire history of our species we have looked up, but we had never been able to look back and see ourselves.

The impact of seeing ourselves on our planet hanging in space cannot be quantified or measured scientifically, but it is very much there, nonetheless. Of course, some people had considered what the effect of seeing the whole Earth from space might have on life on Earth but, in 1968, at the height of the space race, the focus was still very much on heading into a new frontier. Perhaps there was even a failure to imagine how much Earth, and our lives on this planet, could be changed because of space. Yet it turned out that one of the greatest things that space exploration gave us was ... Earth. A new view, a new perspective, perhaps even a new respect for our planet and desire to improve life on Earth – all from looking back at where we come from.

Imagine for a moment you are an astronaut aboard Apollo 8, back in 1968. Imagine looking out of the window and seeing the entire Earth – that is, everything you have ever known and will likely ever know, apart from your own cramped spacecraft – as something so small and distant. Now imagine holding out your hand and covering the Earth with just your thumb – just as the crew of Apollo 8 did. That's the whole of humanity, hidden by your thumb.

When the picture made it back to Earth, many people were struck not just by the sheer beauty of our brilliant blue-and-green planet, but how fragile it looked. We might go to space in pursuit of scientific discovery, or for the technologies that can improve how we do things on Earth, or simply because of our inbuilt human sense of curiosity and adventure, but in so doing we gain a new way of looking at all the problems we collectively face as a planet.

Earthrise came just six years after the seminal book *Silent Spring* by Rachel Carson, which showed how human use of pesticides was severely damaging the natural world, and it contributed to the development of the growing environmental movement at the time. For the first time we could see, with striking clarity, how fragile our planet really is. While the thousands of satellites passing over our heads are a source of invaluable data, going to space has given us the remarkable privilege of looking back and really seeing Earth for the delicate and beautiful thing that it is.

For me, the greatest thing to come from space exploration is not the epic endeavours, it is not the exploration – though these things are hugely important – it is us. Space makes us realise who we really are. And if we don't do much to look after ourselves, our absence will be insignificant within the grandeur of the universe. Earth is ours and we need to look after it.

All the planets and moons in our solar system, and planets around far-away stars, have one thing in common: they are not Earth. So far we have not discovered another planet truly like our own, capable of not only sustaining our species, and all of the other species with which we share our Earthly home, but capable of allowing us to thrive. Going into space gives us the best chance for our species' survival, not because humans are going to move to Mars or the Moon, but because the view from space gives us this new way of seeing the problems we collectively face and a new opportunity to find ways of addressing them.

Our space age is still very much in its infancy. A rocket launch is still a big deal, and there are, relatively speaking, few human-made objects in space. Yet in a short time we have been able to develop space technologies that have transformed life on Earth. Our world of today is truly unrecognisable from the one that humans first left to reach for the stars. And even though we didn't get the space future we imagined, space is still everywhere, and in everything we do. Maybe if you could go back and tell a 1960s child about our unexpected space age, about apps and GPS and connectivity, they'd still want the jetpacks and flying cars. But it has made life so much better. As we continue to explore space, do more research and develop new technologies to help us get there, we will continue to be able to use this platform to benefit Earth.

Chapter Four

WHERE NEXT?

'There are more things in heaven and Earth, Horatio, than are dreamt of in your philosophy.'
William Shakespeare

Part 1 – The Entrepreneurial Space Age

In June 2004, Mike Melvill watched through a series of small round windows as the sky turned from blue to black. The only person aboard SpaceShipOne – a cigar-shaped spacecraft just five feet wide, with short, stubby wings and decorated with stars – he was about to do something only a few hundred people had done before him: travel to space. As he passed an altitude of 100km (62.5 miles) 'up', he crossed an imaginary boundary known as the Kármán Line – the internationally accepted point at which we define space to begin. In doing so, Mike Melvill earned himself the title of astronaut.

Strapped to his seat and wearing his helmet, shades and oxygen mask, he was now in the microgravity environment of space. He popped open a bag of M&Ms and watched as the sweets danced freely around the cockpit. In front of him, separating the coast of California from the darkness of space, the thin blue line of the Earth's atmosphere could be seen arching across our planet. At 63 years old, Mike Melvill had just become the four-hundred-and-thirty-fifth human to experience our Earth in this way. His time in space lasted just minutes; not long after taking in the view, Mike was back where he had started the day, on the ground in the baking desert heat of Mojave, California. But his brief voyage beyond Earth marked a major turning point in the way we explore space.

Mike emerged from SpaceShipOne in front of a huddle of photographers and camera crews, hundreds of journalists and many more spectators, and was met by the maverick aerospace engineer Burt Rutan and the Microsoft co-founder and billionaire Paul Allen. For while being the four-hundred-and-thirty-fifth human to travel to space might not seem remarkable enough to attract such attention, Mike didn't simply return to Earth as an astronaut; he had just become the world's first commercial astronaut.

The flight of SpaceShipOne wasn't a NASA or a military mission. This was something the world had never seen before: the first ever private space mission. This 'day trip to space' had been financed by Paul Allen, who had wanted to invest in low-cost, reusable space transportation and had backed Burt Rutan's design.

SpaceShipOne wasn't a conventional spacecraft but a spaceplane that attached to the belly of a larger 'mothership' aircraft called White Knight. White Knight carried SpaceShipOne to an altitude of 50,000 feet, from where it was released. After a few moments of freefall, SpaceShipOne fired its rocket engines to take it on a path to space. The flight on the morning of 21 June 2004 had been the fifteenth flight of SpaceShipOne, but the first that would take it far enough away from Earth for Mike Melvill to gain his astronaut wings. Paul Allen's wealth and his willingness to take a financial risk, the genius of Burt Rutan's design skills and the bravery of test pilot Mike Mevill had transformed going to space from something which had, until that morning, been the preserve of governments to something that could be achieved by private individuals.

Posing for photographs by the spacecraft, this trio represented what it's going to take to push the boundaries of what we can do in space. Firstly, we need dreamers and mavericks, people such as Burt Rutan, who can go against the status quo and create bold new ideas. Secondly, we need wealthy individuals – those who are willing to stake parts of their fortunes on those ideas, to take financial risks that governments spending public money cannot. And thirdly, we need people who are willing to accept the dangers associated with stepping into the unknown, such as Mike Melvill, because expanding our frontiers is never easy. Lives have been lost in the pursuit of space exploration and, as humans step ever further away from our planet, although we will not do so recklessly, those risks will continue to be there.

In the years since that maiden spaceflight of SpaceShipOne, private companies and ultra-wealthy individuals with extremely deep pockets have taken space from a place to go to a place to do business. The space race first took us to the stars; the unexpected space age gave us our modern world – now, our new era of space exploration is all about the entrepreneur. By the year 2040, according to Morgan Stanley, 'space' is set to become a trillion-dollar industry.

Across the world, there are now numerous commercial space companies – from giant conglomerates bankrolled by billionaires to small start-ups with just a handful of people at the helm, and everything in between. Some of these companies are working alone or with other private space companies; others are working in partnership with government organisations such as NASA. Their goals range from sending tourists and professional astronauts to space, to getting rid of debris left in Earth's orbit, constructing private space stations, manufacturing, mining asteroids and the Moon, providing internet connectivity across our planet and using data gathered from space-based observations of Earth to bring real benefit to people's lives, to name but a few.

The media likes to write headlines about a 'new space race' between high-profile players such as SpaceX and Virgin Galactic. Perhaps because it seems easy to compare what's happening now with the space race of the 1960s and 1970s, and that's the story they associate with space – a contest between two powers, with an ultimate end goal. This sounds exciting, of course, and makes good headlines, but this simply isn't the case. What is happening now is not a race, at least, not one that's comparable to the early years of space exploration. In this entrepreneurial space age there is no single goal, or single focus for what we are doing. Space is limitless and so are our opportunities there. This is not to say there is no competition between businesses pursuing all these new possibilities, but this time there is no finish line – we are not racing to a final destination where we'll plant a flag, take some photos and then not return for 50 years.

Instead, we should compare this new, entrepreneurial space age to the Wild West or – less romantically, perhaps – to the early internet era of the 1990s. In some ways it's a free-for-all, a new platform to dream up crazy ideas and try them out. Not only are there opportunities to improve and make money from the existing things for which we use space, such as Earth observations and communications, but new companies and ideas will disrupt the world in ways we haven't even thought of yet. Think about how the internet gave us companies such as Facebook and Amazon, and how the innovations they introduced profoundly changed how we communicate and shop in ways we could never have imagined at their inception. Just like these businesses, the new commercial space companies are trying to develop their own product or service and make it the best it can be, and perhaps to corner a market that doesn't even exist yet.

The coming years will see a shift in our perception of what it means to go to space and what we are doing there. Going into space is about extending our presence beyond Earth, expanding the horizons of where we exist and pushing forward as a species into the wider solar system – while at the same time continuing to use the vantage point of space to improve life on Earth. It is a complex task, bigger than any one person or country, and there need to be many players. Not just to meet the technological challenges, but also in how we regulate this new frontier.

Doing business in space will undoubtedly raise some big questions – the biggest one being 'who owns space?' Can any individual or a country stake a claim to a particular area of space, like explorers and prospectors did on Earth in the past? This is something we have considered since we first started exploring space. In 1967, the UN Outer Space Treaty was signed. It was designed to provide the legal framework for how nations should behave, declaring that while countries and individuals are entitled to 'fair use', no one nation can lay claim to anywhere in space. It's now been signed by more than 100 countries. In the US in 2015, the Commercial Space Launch Competitiveness Act was passed, allowing US citizens to extract resources from space, but preventing them from laying claim to any body in the solar system. The reality, though, is that this is something that is continually changing, and in extending our presence beyond Earth, the regulation can only develop alongside what we are doing.

So where does this lead us? As businesses figure out how to make money from going into space, we'll move closer and closer towards an 'off-world economy'. Companies might even one day operate solely in space, selling to other space-based businesses. Of course, the idea of expanding humanity's presence beyond Earth and creating an off-world economy sounds impossible now, but so did the world we live in today just a matter of decades ago. Everything we do is constantly pushing the limits of what was thought to be possible.

Mike Melvill's second spaceflight aboard SpaceShipOne in autumn 2004 was followed by the spacecraft's third and final flight five days later, this time flown by another test pilot, called Brian Binnie. These flights were hugely significant: a private company going to space wasn't just a one-off, it was something that was potentially sustainable. The less-than-two-week gap between these spaceflights was significant, for that was part of the terms of the Ansari X Prize – a prize designed to help incentivise the development of lower-cost, reusable and privately developed space travel. The team behind SpaceShipOne won the prize, receiving a reward of $10 million – although this money did not come close to covering the cost of what had been spent on the project.

The idea of wealthy companies and individuals providing an incentive to spur on explorers and adventurers to see what we are capable of is not a recent invention. Offering prizes to reward those who take risks and push the boundaries has a long and interesting history, particularly in the field of aviation. The most famous example, one that helped to inspire the Ansari X Prize, was the wealthy New York hotelier Raymond Orteig, who in 1919 put up a $25,000 reward for whoever could complete the world's first non-stop solo transatlantic flight, as a 'stimulus for courageous aviators'. It was eight years before anyone could achieve this feat, but then, in May 1927, Charles Lindbergh landed his plane, the *Spirit of St Louis*, in Paris, 33 hours after taking off from New York, and won the prize. While many failed in their pursuit, that one successful flight by Charles Lindbergh changed everything, helping to lay the foundations for the development of transatlantic flight, which we today take for granted. So in many ways, what we are doing in space is nothing new. The only thing that's different is the playing field.

The world's first successful aeroplane – the *Wright Flyer* – lives in the Smithsonian Air and Space Museum in Washington, DC. It shares its home with Lindberg's *Spirit of St Louis* and now with SpaceShipOne. All three craft represent something which was once seen as impossible but is now consigned to our history books. They show how our achievements are becoming ever more sophisticated, and symbolise how our imagination and risk-taking led us to the world we live in today.

Among the key players in this new, entrepreneurial space age are some of the wealthiest on our planet, people who are often prepared to personally invest sometimes huge amounts of money in this new frontier, on things that have never been done before. There are also often mavericks, people from all kinds of backgrounds, who are daring to dream really bold ideas – ideas that sometimes people scoff at because they sound so impossible.

Two of the highest-profile space entrepreneurs and innovators are Elon Musk and Jeff Bezos. Both are self-made, highly intelligent people, who made their vast fortunes in the dotcom boom of the 1990s. These men spotted the opportunities made available by the early internet era and now they are focusing on the possibilities that are to come from looking up. Musk's ultimate ambitions extend to seeing humans on Mars; Bezos wants to pave the way for future generations in space, effectively setting up an infrastructure which will facilitate lower-cost frequent access to space for future generations. Of the two, it is Elon Musk who courts the most attention from the media – not all of it positive, but then space exploration has never been a popularity contest.

On a warm February afternoon in 2018 at NASA's Kennedy Space Center in Florida, I watched as Musk's Falcon Heavy rocket roared through the blue cloudless sky, looking like a bright candle in the distance. The thing about launches is that you don't just see them, you feel them; you literally experience the roar of the rocket travelling through the air as it leaves our planet. Aboard the Falcon Heavy on its maiden voyage was a special payload – not astronauts, nor a robotic craft going to explore unchartered parts of our solar system, but Elon Musk's very own cherry red Tesla. In the driver's seat sat a dummy wearing a spacesuit. Back on Earth, in Florida, David Bowie's 'Starman' was blasted through speakers as the successful launch of the most powerful rocket to fly since the Saturn V (which was used to take humans to the Moon) was celebrated. Not long after, the first images from space arrived; onboard cameras allowed us to see the cherry red Tesla, with the dummy in the spacesuit – aptly named 'Starman' – in space, with our Earth, and all of us, behind it.

We were looking at the greatest car advert of all time. But this wasn't just a billionaire recklessly sending his car into space for a thrill. When you launch new types of rockets for the first time, you generally have to have a 'test payload' on board. This is something that essentially acts as a weight in place of something more valuable. After all, this *is* rocket science and things can go wrong, so companies or organisations often aren't willing to risk expensive equipment or spacecraft on test flights. However, the choice of the car with the 'dummy' passenger was a genius PR move, as the story of Starman riding his Tesla through space was reported worldwide. The photographs captivated people in a way that had not been seen in a long time. And all of a sudden, people were talking about space. There is even to this day a website where you can track Starman in his Tesla on his journey around our Sun, in an orbit which places him between the Earth and Mars, where this unlikely spaceship and its passenger will remain for a long time to come.

Just over two years later, in May 2020, SpaceX's Crew Dragon launched two astronauts into space for the first time, making them the first private company to do so for NASA. As part of NASA's Commercial Crew Programme – alongside Boeing and its Starliner craft – SpaceX, using its Crew Dragon capsule and its smaller Falcon 9 rocket, are taking crew to the International

Space Station, along with supplies to enable NASA to focus its efforts on returning humans to the Moon, under its Artemis Program.

Elon Musk founded SpaceX in 2002 to revolutionise our current space technology. Among the company's goals are getting to space more effectively and at a lower cost. Many thousands of people work at the company, dedicating their lives to disrupting the way we do things in space, but at the helm of SpaceX is engineer and businesswoman Gwynne Shotwell. Voted one of the most powerful women in the world by *Forbes*, it is she who is responsible for turning Musk's bold vision into reality.

Musk believes that, if we are to survive as a species, humans need to get to the planet Mars. And not just to visit, but to create a self-sustaining community. If something disastrous happens on Earth, Musk reasons that having humans on Mars would ensure there is enough of a 'seed of civilization somewhere else' to allow our species to continue. What this ambition is not, is a case of wanting to go to Mars and forget about Earth, as occasionally gets misreported.

This desire to go into space for the good of our species is something that also motivates Jeff Bezos, the Amazon billionaire whose space company Blue Origin began its existence in the year 2000, largely operating behind closed doors. Whereas Musk's SpaceX is essentially a government contractor, providing launches for NASA, Bezos's Blue Origin had been solely funded by the billionaire himself, who sells $100 million in Amazon shares each year to bankroll it. Bezos simply doesn't need the same level of publicity when he doesn't rely on government contracts or investors.

Although Bezos is the richest person in the world, he came from humble beginnings, born to a teenage mum, with his biological father leaving them when he was just months old. Bezos has been fascinated by space and the benefits it could bring to Earth since he was a child. As valedictorian at his high school graduation in 1982, he talked then of his plans to take many more humans to space, and Blue Origin is trying to do just that, working under the motto *gradatim ferociter*, Latin for 'step by step, ferociously'.

Bezos's vision for the future is to use space to protect Earth, looking at moving manufacturing away from our planet and using the abundant resources that exist in space instead of exploiting those on Earth. He envisages millions of people living and working in space, eventually making humans a multi-planetary species. As Bezos puts it, 'There are currently 7.6 billion people on Earth, but if space becomes a viable place for humans to live, the solar system has enough resources to support 1 trillion humans. Then we'd have 1,000 Mozarts and 1,000 Einsteins.' While that won't happen within our lifetime, his hope is that the work he is doing today will pave the way for future generations to realise this ambition. The motivation behind this? To help us move forward into space, to start this incredible journey into the universe and in doing so look after Earth. The projects that Blue Origin are currently working on include reducing the cost of both orbital and sub-orbital flights, space tourism and working alongside other companies to develop the lunar lander for the Artemis Program. Finding better, more efficient ways of doing things we have done before.

I once worked with Bezos, interviewing him on stage in Seattle, in front of a crowd that included Bill Gates, Warren Buffett and the Canadian Prime Minister Justin Trudeau, among other dignitaries – some of the most powerful people in the world who had come together to hear about space. Afterwards I gave Bezos a poem which had been given to me by an engineer who had worked on the Apollo missions to the Moon. Many of those who dedicated their lives to the Apollo missions, to seeing humans on the Moon, felt disappointed that we had not yet returned. This poem, called 'Where Is Our Purpose Now?', talked of how instead of looking back to the space race and what had been achieved in the past, we should focus on the future, for that is where our purpose lies. There was no better person I could think to give it to than Jeff Bezos. The Apollo generation made the work of Blue Origin possible, just as Bezos hopes his work will contribute to the achievements in space of future generations.

In the past, anyone who wanted to work in the space industry had to do so at either a government organisation or a major aerospace corporation, such as Lockheed Martin or Boeing, to name but two, but now that is no longer the case. While this doesn't mean that everyone can have their own rocket ship company just yet – we still need governments and ultra-wealthy individuals to get us to space – what it does mean is that having ideas about space and working to develop businesses around them are no longer the preserve of the few. In many ways, it is similar to what happened when Europeans started to explore our own Earth. The analogy I like to draw is that Apollo can almost be thought of as a 'Columbus moment' in terms of exploration, while this new era in space is comparable to the voyage of the *Mayflower*. Just like the Moon landings, Columbus's voyage to the Americas was funded by a government in order to gain supremacy over another country. So perhaps we can compare privately funded space flights to the *Mayflower* setting sail for the New World.

With all this opportunity for new ideas and business, there is of course the potential for vast amounts of money to be made. Much of that money in the short term will come from using space-based technology to look back at Earth and provide information and services. But you will be hard pushed to find anyone in this new generation of space entrepreneurs who is motivated solely by money. There are easier fields in which to make a fortune than the new frontier of commercial space ventures, and many investors will lose everything. A fascination with space travel and a desire to be part of pushing into a new frontier is likely to be an equally important motivation.

But even when they are not successful, these companies will help drive forward the space industry; they will show us what will not work, and how we can learn from it. We don't yet know exactly what technology we will need as we figure out how to stay for longer and do business in space. No doubt this generation and the next of space entrepreneurs will invent their own equivalents to the jetpack of the 1960s – a scientific novelty that future generations will look back on and smile. But there is no such thing as failing when you are pushing open a new frontier, just ways of learning how to do things better. To quote the inventor Thomas Edison, 'I didn't fail, I just found 10,000 ideas that won't work.'

Some entrepreneurs are focusing on improving the technology we already have. At NASA's Johnson Space Center in Houston, I tried on a bright orange spacesuit and attempted to re-pressurise my ears as it was filled with air. But this wasn't a NASA spacesuit. It had been designed by a startup company with the goal of creating affordable spacesuits in anticipation of more people being able to travel to space in the future. This is just one example of how, in this entrepreneurial space age, new space companies are trying to find innovative, more efficient and less expensive ways of doing everything we already do in space. This isn't a case of reinventing the wheel; it is about anticipating what we are going to need as space travel becomes more accessible. What demands will there be? And how can entrepreneurs be ready to meet those needs? Unlike governments and large corporations, startups are able to take more risks in their designs and ideas. They are effectively creating the technology we will need tomorrow, today, while applying the famous Silicon Valley mentality of 'move fast and break things'.

In 2016, astronaut Jeff Williams and cosmonaut Oleg Skripochka became the first humans to enter an expandable habitat in space. Wearing face masks, they opened the hatch of the International Space Station – to which this new invention was attached – and floated inside, gathering air samples and leaving sensors to collect data.

While this might not seem like a momentous occasion for space exploration, the Bigelow Expandable Activity Module (BEAM) could have huge implications for where future humans can live in space. The ISS is made up of a collection of solid modules, built and designed on Earth, launched into space and then attached together in orbit; it took 30 space missions and ten years to assemble. But BEAM is different; it is essentially a pop-up tent, which takes up far less room when it is launched and is later expanded in space. The idea was originally developed by NASA in the 1960s, but after the project was cancelled the rights were bought by a private company called Bigelow Aerospace, founded by the billionaire businessman Robert Bigelow. Bigelow made his fortune in hotels, but his passion is for space, and he has dedicated part of his wealth to changing how we build habitats in space in the future. These 'pop-up tents' could be used to construct future bases on the Moon, for example, in place of bulky modules.

Others are looking at things we already do on Earth and asking how we could do them in space. The goal of

Astrobotic is to create the first lunar delivery service for future space missions. Think of this as a robotic DHL, but for the Moon – although it's unlikely they'd be able to leave your parcel with a neighbour! In the near term, this could mean delivering everything from experiments to personal mementos to the Moon. There is growing interest in 'space funerals', with people wanting their ashes scattered in space, as well as personal items. In the longer term, it could deliver parcels and equipment to future astronauts on the Moon's surface.

Of course, while these innovations will have a big impact on our future in space, it's human space travel that really captures our imagination. Among those watching the third and final flight of SpaceShipOne was Richard Branson. Following the success of these missions, Burt Rutan went on to design a larger version of his craft, this time backed financially by Branson, and known as SpaceShipTwo. Today, SpaceShipTwo is used by Virgin Galactic for its short passenger trips to space. What started as a competition to become the first privately funded space mission has led to a way for potentially many more people to leave Earth, even if it is just for a matter of minutes. And while these first few tourist trips are short (and expensive!), they are helping to make space accessible to many more people. This, combined with much of the work being done by other companies, is helping to lay the foundations of humans extending their presence beyond Earth.

When historians look back at our time, they will see

what we are doing in space today as a pivot point, one that took us from visiting space to extending our presence beyond Earth. All the bold ideas, the failures and risks are paving the way for this. What we are doing now is our gift to the future.

Part 2 – Leaving Earth

For all our ambitions, the fact remains that leaving planet Earth is not so easy. One of the main reasons why more of us have not gone to space is because the act of stepping away from Earth is rather complex. The principles behind every launch and the act of going 'up' are relatively simple, governed by Isaac Newton's third law: every action requires an equal and opposite reaction. But being able to actually escape Earth's gravity is less so.

In order to get to space you need to achieve what is known as escape velocity. Escape velocity is essentially the speed at which an object (such as your spacecraft) must be travelling in order to break free of Earth's gravity. To leave our planet and to get into orbit – achieving a height of some 140 miles up – you need to travel at a speed of at least seven miles per second. To put it another way, that is 25,000mph. When you look at those numbers, you can understand why travelling what appears to be a relatively short distance can be so complex. To get to that speed you need a lot of fuel, but the more fuel you have the more you weigh. The more you weigh, the more fuel you need to lift you. This is hugely expensive, plus, to date, many of the rockets we have used to get there have been essentially 'thrown away' afterwards – they have only been able to be used once. But if we want to push forward into space, we need to figure out a better way of getting there.

You wouldn't throw away your car after a single journey, so why throw away a space rocket? The idea of reusing space vehicles is nothing new. NASA's Space Shuttle was designed to be reusable, with the orbiter (that's the part where the astronauts sit, which looks a bit like a plane) and the boosters on the side designed so they could be repaired and used again after a flight. However, the Space Shuttle was very complex and became much more expensive than anticipated. So although we had a spacecraft and rocket boosters that could be used again and again, by the time they were serviced and prepared for their next flight, the cost was so huge that no money had really been saved. The average shuttle mission cost $450 million.

Among those trying to solve the problem of reusable space vehicles are our two entrepreneurial space age heavyweights, Jeff Bezos and Elon Musk. They are able to try things government agencies – tied up in questions of funding and subsequent politics – cannot, taking more risks and experimenting with new ideas. They are of course aided by our advances in technology – the Space Shuttle was designed and built in the 1970s and kept flying space missions until 2011. Musk hopes that creating cheaper, reusable space transportation will help achieve his plan of sending humans to Mars. Whereas for Bezos, lower-cost launches are in line with his ambitions of more people being able to access space.

Because going to space is so expensive, there is a high bar to entry, meaning while there are plenty of people with ideas, few can actually get those ideas to space to test them out. Getting to space isn't ever going to be free, but a significant reduction in its cost will mean more companies and entrepreneurs are able to gain access for their ideas, experiments and satellites. It's not dissimilar to the way that the internet enabled students to create world-changing companies from their dorm rooms with few overheads.

So how does making rockets reusable work? A rocket is generally made up of different stages. The most common type is a two-stage rocket used to get payloads to orbit. The first stage is the lower part of the rocket, that gets us above most of the 'air'. This is where we need the most fuel, as there is more resistance. Once it has done its job, it is discarded and falls back to Earth, where, in many cases, it will come to rest on the bottom of the ocean (no floating wreckage is allowed). The second stage then gives the payload (be that astronauts or a satellite) the final 'boost' it needs to escape Earth's gravity. In most cases, this second stage then burns up in the Earth's atmosphere. Millions of dollars and many thousands of hours of work are gone in a matter of seconds.

Both SpaceX and Blue Origin are finding ways to land the rocket parts back on Earth instead of discarding them.

In December 2015, SpaceX made history when its Falcon 9 rocket's discarded first stage landed back on Earth after helping to successfully put a series of satellites in orbit. It was an incredible feat of engineering, with the booster slowing it down to softly touch down on a landing pad not far from where it had launched only minutes earlier. Today this is something associated with nearly every SpaceX launch.

After successfully landing back on Earth – on either a landing pad or a specially designed barge in the ocean – the parts of the rocket are then refurbished and used for other missions. The goal is for SpaceX to be able to recover and reuse the entire rocket, with the aim of reducing the cost of their launches from around $60 million to $6 million. At Blue Origin, a similar technique is used, again using boosters to slow and safely land their rockets back on Earth after launch. Step by step, with each mission, they are perfecting these landings.

Another way of reducing the cost of launching humans or equipment into space is through the use of lighter-weight materials, so that less fuel is needed to break free of the Earth's gravity, and a number of companies that have been around for many decades are doing just that. Advances in technology also mean that satellites have become smaller and lighter in weight, which also helps to reduce the cost of getting them to space.

There are also other methods of getting satellites to space than starting with a rocket on the ground and taking off vertically – such as launching from either an aeroplane or a balloon high up in the sky. From this position you are above much of the atmosphere, meaning you need less fuel to get to space. This idea was first used in the late 1940s with experimental aircraft and is now being employed today. While Richard Branson's Virgin Galactic is only capable of making short journeys to space – not high enough to reach orbit or the space station – its sister company, Virgin Orbit, is among those using aeroplanes to send satellites into orbit. As satellites become less expensive, more people will be able to access their on-Earth benefits.

What we will see in our space future is a change to the way we get to space, both for sending people as well as ideas and experiments. While witnessing a rocket launch and then part of it landing back on Earth just minutes later may be a novelty today, I look forward to the day that this becomes ordinary, and no different to seeing a car, a plane or a train.

But once we've improved how we get to space, there will be more hurdles to overcome. Some are problems of our own making. When we first went to space, we didn't think of the consequences of our actions. Scattered among the satellites that orbit our planet are hundreds of thousands of pieces of junk, from small fragments less than a centimetre in size, to astronaut gloves and bits of old spacecraft. Travelling at thousands of miles an hour around our planet, space junk is a very real issue, posing the threat of collisions with the satellites we rely on as well as astronauts aboard the space station. Whereas today there are methods in place to de-orbit satellites, by either having them burn up in our atmosphere or placed in a graveyard orbit, we still need – just like on Earth – to do something about the existing mess we have left behind. It only takes one collision between two pieces of space junk to create yet more debris in its aftermath. If we want to continue going into space, we need to clean up after ourselves.

The next step is making space an extension of life on Earth. By this, I mean learning to do many of the things we do on Earth in the harsh environment of space. This will be a big step in giving us the capability to travel further away from Earth. But first we need to have less of a dependence on Earth-based resources – this is the real key to enabling us to send people further out into the solar system, and this is where many more companies and individuals with new ideas come into play. To start to live in space – beyond the International Space Station, that is – we are going to need new tools and techniques.

For example, we need to learn how to 'live off the land' and become self-sustaining. When we explored and set- tled in different areas of the Earth, the pioneers didn't bring everything they needed with them; they adapted to their surroundings. We need to be able to do this in space. At present, astronauts aboard the International Space Station are dependent on resupply ships from Earth bringing everything from replacement tools to food and medical supplies. This is fine for astronauts in orbit around our planet – and a reduction in the cost of launch in the future would in theory make it easier to send supplies to astronauts – but if we want to go further into space, we need to learn how to survive without these constant resupplies.

In 1970, as the crew of Apollo 13 was on the way to the Moon, there was an explosion that caused a rupture of one of the craft's oxygen tanks. This crippled the Command and Service Module that the crew were in, resulting in the three astronauts having to power it down and take shelter in the Lunar Module in order to survive. However, the Lunar Module was only designed for two people, and with three people now using it, the filters were unable to cope, which meant carbon dioxide levels increased. The solution to this problem was to take the carbon dioxide filters from the Command Module and use them in the Lunar Module. Sounds simple enough, however the problem was that the filters on the Command Module were round and the ones on the Lunar Module were square. The team in Mission Control was left essentially trying to work out how to fit a square peg into a round hole using just the material the crew had available to them in space.

You probably know the ending of this tale – Mission Control worked out how to solve the problem using a makeshift contraption fashioned from materials on board and the crew survived. Now, let's reimagine the story, with the crew having a 3D printer with them – one more advanced than what we have today, but technology that is certainly within the realms of possibility for our future. The crew could have simply 'printed' the part they needed while in space. Of course, it would have made less of an exciting scene in the Hollywood movie some years later, but being able to manufacture things in space, to do all the things we do on Earth, without Earth, is our next step in enabling us to no longer reside on just one planet.

This sounds like science fiction, but it's happening now. Aboard the International Space Station is a 3D printer designed to work in the microgravity environment of space, owned by a private company called Made in Space, which is trying to do just that. Make things in space. And it's already starting to happen. One astronaut on the ISS – Butch Wilmore – lost his ratchet during a spacewalk. An easy enough thing to do, to drop a tool while you're working on a piece of equipment. But in space, there's no way to get it back. But whereas once they would have had to wait for a resupply ship, something that could take months, Wilmore was able to make a new ratchet on the space station using the 3D printer.

The possibilities to come from manufacturing in space are almost as endless as the possibilities to come from space itself, and the less expensive and easier getting to space becomes, the more progress we can make towards learning how to do this. Everything from medical supplies to habitats could one day be created in space. Instead of making things on Earth, then launching and sometimes assembling them in space, we could create something where and when we need it. As both technology and our exploration of space evolve, one day we could arrive at a 'new world', somewhere else within our solar system or perhaps even beyond, and be able to 3D-print everything we need from the land on which we find ourselves. It's not possible yet, but it could be in the future.

This type of manufacturing in space will even potentially improve the construction of the satellites we have already come to rely on. Currently satellites have to endure the stresses of being launched into space, so they have inbuilt support structures that help to withstand this, but these are then redundant once the satellite reaches space. But manufacturing in space means we'll be able to send up the raw materials and assemble better, more efficient satellites with bolder designs. This is something companies are working on right now, and in the future we could see whole assembly plants in space, creating satellites to look back at Earth that we will continue to rely on every day. The skills used to assemble satellites in space could even be used to repair existing satellites, instead of astronauts having to perform risky spacewalks.

While manufacturing might not sound like the most exciting aspect of space exploration, changing the way we do everyday things and learning how to do them away from Earth is what is going to help drive us forward in space. Getting food to eat, without being reliant on Earth, is another huge challenge; plants, much like people, aren't really designed for spaceflight. It is a problem that is being tackled by both government agencies and individual companies. The first astronauts we sent into space were hardened military personnel, with the technical skills to pilot spacecraft and the training to cope with the risks associated with this brand-new technology. Now, the type of person we send to space is changing. As we learn to do new things in space, we need people with skills in areas such as growing crops.

Other companies and countries are looking at the possibilities of mining in space. While this seems like a bold new idea, it is again no different to what we have done on Earth – harnessing the resources available. The prospect of mining in space offers not only the potential to provide more resources for Earth, but a way to enable exploring further into space, without relying on our finite resources on this planet.

We know that frozen water is prevalent throughout our solar system; there is evidence of it at the poles on the Moon and in asteroids, both in the asteroid belt (between the planets Mars and Jupiter) and on those that pass closer to Earth. Water is important for many reasons, other than just simply keeping us alive. The key ingredients of the fuel used in liquid rocket engines are hydrogen and oxygen. And, as we know, water, be it frozen or liquid, is made up of hydrogen and oxygen (H_2O). So some of our nearest cosmic neighbours have the ingredients we need to create rocket fuel. You could almost think of a small part of the Moon as one day having the facilities for a space-based 'petrol station' for rocket fuel. In theory, instead of having to launch with a huge amount of fuel – enough to get us where we want to go – we could instead 'fill up' at the Moon or an asteroid before heading deeper into the solar system. Mining for frozen water is merely another step towards using resources we can find in space rather than having to take them with us, and this will help future space explorers survive beyond Earth.

The potential of space mining doesn't just stop at frozen water. Minerals that are rare and precious on Earth are common in parts of the solar system. For example, cobalt – an element that's found in lithium ion batteries, which are used in everything from your smartphone to laptops and electric vehicles – can be found in many asteroids throughout our solar system. On Earth, around 60 per cent of the cobalt we need for the batteries that power our devices comes from the Democratic Republic of the Congo (DRC). This is a country I have seen first-hand, a place where four out of five people live in extreme poverty, and one of the most violent regions of our planet. What I saw in its city of Goma felt like the gateway to hell. Elsewhere in the country there are reports of children digging with their hands in mines, wearing no protective clothing. This is the grim reality behind much of our modern technology.

In the short term, I can't claim that mining in space is a solution for those problems in places like the DRC, particularly as demand for electric vehicles (and the cobalt needed for the batteries) increases. We're a long way off being able to mine minerals in space for commercial use. Yet, in the future, if we are able to get these resources from space – and not just cobalt, but the many other precious metals and materials which are so in demand in our changing world – instead of mining our planet, instead of having children in horrendous conditions work underground for the key ingredients to the technology we are so reliant on, we could one day take the resources we need robotically from the abundant supply that exists within our solar system.

While we are working to address changes to the demand for resources on Earth, mining in space is not about 'going to another planet to ruin it, just like we have ruined the Earth', as some mistake this for. Mining is a way of utilising the resources available away from Earth to help us as we explore further, while also potentially benefiting life on Earth.

One of the ways to get over the many hurdles we face in learning how to exist beyond Earth is by returning to the Moon. But what we will see next are not short missions, as with Apollo, but missions of a much longer duration, with humans living and working on the Moon, much like what has been done on the ISS in Earth orbit. The Moon, roughly a three-day trip away, is the natural next step. It can very much be thought of as a stepping stone, a place where we can send people to stay on a lunar base for extended periods of time – weeks or even months – to test out all the technology we need to go further into space. But it's also close enough to home should there be any issues.

The Apollo missions were on the lunar surface for only a matter of hours – Apollo 17 was there the longest, but still astronauts Gene Cernan and Jack Schmitt spent only 75 hours there. This was just enough time to gather some samples, take photos and begin to explore the area around where they had landed. But a return to the Moon would be more than just flags and footprints. It is about building a sustainable human presence with the long-term goal of a lunar base. The International Space Station has enabled us to learn how to live and work in space, as well as to find out what happens to the human body when we spend long periods of time in microgravity. We also needed to demonstrate that the potential advantages to be gained from space go beyond just exploration, so that more people would invest in the idea of going there. And the world of cyberspace – the internet era that came from the 1990s – gave us a new generation of entrepreneurs who are now concentrating their efforts in space, and a new generation of investors, who saw success stories from investing in early-stage companies and seemingly crazy ideas. Imagine if you had bought shares in Amazon or Netflix 15 years ago – you'd probably be more willing to bet on a bold new space company.

And most importantly, we have learned how to work together in space. Much of what we have achieved so far has been the result of collaboration, not just between scientists and engineers, but between different countries and private companies. One of the greatest successes of the International Space Station has been exactly this type of collaboration in pursuit of a common goal. What we are doing in space is beyond any one nation or company – it is far too complex for that. And while a return of humans to the Moon may be led by NASA under its Artemis Program, staying there long term will require collaboration as much as competition.

Once on the Moon, astronauts will build on the skills we have developed living aboard the space station. The Moon has the added advantage of having gravity, although it's only one-sixth as strong as on Earth – this is something which is significant, because if we want to go further into space, to visit other planets, the Moon can act as an analogue for future deeper-space missions. We have to slowly edge out into space. Everything from new rovers, to spacesuits, to the psychological impact of being further away from home can be studied in detail.

There is also a huge amount of science which can be conducted on the Moon. With every step forward in space, we are essentially gathering more pieces of the 'jigsaw puzzle' to try to piece together an understanding of our own existence. Our Moon can be thought of as a time capsule from the early solar system. Unlike our Earth's surface, which is constantly churned and reshaped, the Moon's surface has not changed. Many of the craters are some three billion years old. Studying the Moon gives us a better idea of what happened to our young Earth, as well as providing potential clues as to how life came to be.

And, of course, there is something that cannot quite be measured – the impact on our society and inspiration that comes from seeing humans set foot on another world. Imagine going outside and looking up at the Moon, and knowing there are people there who are looking back at the Earth and all of us. It is a profound thought and one that the majority of our species has not experienced. We have nearly lost the Apollo generation, those who made the first missions to the Moon possible. Today the sad reality is that Apollo is pretty much consigned to our history books – it's something we learn about, and something an ever-decreasing percentage of the world's population bore witness to. Now, with all our advances in modern communications, humans landing on the surface of the Moon would be a very different experience for those of us back home. Television broadcast in high definition. Social media posts. Astronauts on the Moon linking up for live chats into classrooms, major sporting events or even awards shows. Through the likes of NASA, SpaceX, Blue Origin, Boeing, Lockheed Martin, ULA and many other companies and countries, these ambitions are being created. Our future is happening right now.

It was the generation inspired by Apollo who built the modern world – what will those inspired by the next Moon landing create for our future?

Part 3 – Beyond the Moon

While not the closet planet to us (that's Venus), Mars is the planet you would prefer to visit. Venus has a choking thick atmosphere that would crush you and your spacecraft within seconds, while Mars is a lot more pleasant by comparison, although still not a place you could survive without a spacesuit.

Humans have been fascinated by Mars, the 'Red Planet', for as long as we have been looking up. From Earth, even without a telescope, you can make out Mars's reddish hue, as it hangs like a star in the night sky. Romans called it Mars after their god of war, and they took the idea from the Greeks, who had originally named the planet Ares after their god of war. During the late nineteenth century, up to the turn of the twentieth century, after astronomers identified what seemed to be 'canal-like features', some people believed that these were artificially created; before robotic spacecraft began visiting in the 1970s, there was even speculation that there could be intelligent life there.

Today, we know Mars is in some ways a 'dead planet', in the sense that it has no protective magnetic field (Earth's magnetic field is what protects us from the solar wind – charged particles coming from the Sun and the cause of the auroras seen at high latitudes). As a result, Mars has a much thinner atmosphere, after much of it was stripped away by solar winds. Its surface – red because of rust in the soil – is dry and arid, with intense dust storms, some of which are so big they can be seen through telescopes from Earth. Even the planet's volcanoes, which include the largest in our solar system, are dead. By our best scientific estimates, the 600km-wide behemoth Olympus Mons hasn't erupted in 25 million years.

Yet despite this, there are resemblances to Earth in Mars's landscape. It is a rocky world, with mountains and valleys. Running across the planet like a scar is the

Valles Marineris, and though it's wider than the United States, this is Mars's own version of the Grand Canyon. From the surface, the Sun appears around two-thirds of the size that it does when seen from Earth. The sky is pink, and as the Sun sets over this barren, rocky horizon, the sky turns to shades of blue. A blue sunset on an alien world.

The planet is circled by two moons, though they aren't large and inviting like our own Moon. Instead they are tiny and oddly shaped, airless, rocky worlds. Phobos and Deimos, at just 13 and 7.5 miles wide respectively, are most likely asteroids captured by the planet's gravity during the formation of our solar system. They are so small that even seen through our most powerful telescopes on Earth, they just appear as points of light. If you could look up from the surface of Mars at night, depending on your location, these two tiny moons would just look like bright stars traversing the night sky. You would, of course, also see stars – you'd be able to make out the same constellations that you can from going outside and looking up from here on Earth.

A day on Mars is only slightly longer than a day on Earth – 24 hours, 37 minutes and 22 seconds. However, a Martian year lasts 687 Earth days. Mars is colder than Earth – the warmest place is along the equator, where temperatures can reach up to 20 degrees Celsius, but at night, with no thick atmosphere to act as a blanket, temperatures plummet to around -73 degrees Celsius. Like Earth, Mars has seasons; in spring its frozen polar ice caps recede.

While Earth became our blue oasis flushed with life, Mars ended up very different. Yet Mars is still a place of wonder that has been capturing the imaginations of scientists, philosophers, poets and many others for generations. Because of its proximity to us, and the fact that it is the most hospitable world to humans after Earth, Mars is our next natural step into the solar system.

One day we will watch on television – online or through whatever form of media we then use – as a crew leaves our planet bound for Mars. Their journey will take six months or so across the darkness of space. We will watch as the crew approaches Mars, seeing the first photographs of another planet ever taken close-up by humans. We will witness their spacecraft touch down on the surface, and then the hatch door open as the first human being sets foot on the rusty red Martian soil, having completed the most daring and arduous journey ever made, the culmination of eons of difficult human voyages, each one bolder and more daring than the last. In that moment everything changes – we will no longer be confined to just one planet.

As you read this, there may well be a young person, studying in school right now, who will be the first of our kind to ever take in these sights on Mars. The first human being to set foot on another world, another planet, could be alive today. They are a young child who may be inspired by all the adventures we are beginning to have in space. They might be learning about Mars and the other planets in our solar system and the wider universe at school. Or maybe, like me, and countless others, they will simply be inspired by looking up and wondering. But regardless, our first Mars explorers are probably among us.

It is our desire to explore, to answer questions, to push the limits of what we are capable of and – for some – to secure our future that drives us to Mars. Put simply, why would you want to stay still, stay confined to this one world, when there is a whole universe out there waiting to be discovered? We have the potential to do this; it is within our reach. From my point of view we have to go, we have to see what is out there, and Mars is the next step. Maybe we won't live to see what happens after a Mars landing, but to remain still and not try to explore would in many ways be a travesty.

One day, we will be able to look at Mars with the knowledge that there are people there looking back at us. Humans would then be spread between two distant worlds, but they would still look up at the same stars.

Mars is a world full of more questions than answers. Current evidence suggests that it was once much warmer and wetter and its atmosphere was much thicker. But we don't know what happened to Mars. And we also don't know whether we could follow the same fate here on Earth. The planet may have had the conditions for life to have existed in the past. (There may even be microbial life on Mars today.) Life on Earth could have originated from Mars, with our young Earth being seeded by a meteorite from the planet when the solar system was much younger. *We* could be the Martians that science fiction has been searching for, but we probably won't know the answers until we start to send people there.

Although robotic spacecraft are currently on the surface og Mars, they are no substitute for human eyes and dexterity. Robots cover such a small fraction of the planet that it's like landing on Earth on a small island and from there trying to figure out everything about our world. Humans on the surface of Mars will continue the work of robots, looking for evidence of past life, and evidence of current microbial life. Imagine being the person on Mars who finds that clinching piece of evidence we need to conclusively say, yes, there is life on Mars.

If we do discover that there is, or was, life on Mars, and that it evolved independently from Earth, then we will know that there have been two genesis events within our solar system. That there is life independent of Earth and we are not alone. Couple that with our knowledge that the universe is teeming with solar systems, then the probability that there is yet more life out there increases significantly.

The vastness of space is sometimes compared to how people once perceived the great oceans of Earth. Going to Mars is like stepping out from the shore and sailing beyond the horizon for the first time. The voyage, like all voyages of discovery, won't be an easy one. It is likely that people will give their lives for it along the way. And there are many hurdles we face in getting to Mars; crews travelling through deep space will face high levels of radiation and there isn't yet a rocket powerful enough to take people there. And, of course, we will need to master surviving away from Earth. But for all the problems a future human Mars mission faces, there are people working on them.

While Wernher von Braun had plans for a Mars mission in the 1970s, there wasn't the desire politically. But a future mission to Mars will require more than just one country, or company, working alone. And while astronauts may still proudly wear their national flags, they will go to Mars for Earth. Our endeavours in space are too great, too bold, too daring to be done alone.

Get to Mars and we open the gates for future generations to travel even further.

But where we will go next is not yet clear. There are still so many hurdles to overcome. If we want to go further, to the far reaches of our solar system and beyond, we will need new ways of travelling faster. But there is an eternity of wonders awaiting us. Even if we don't find evidence of life on Mars, there are still many other places that may harbour life, even within our own solar system after the Moon.

Orbiting the planet Jupiter is an icy moon called Europa. It has a frozen surface beneath which evidence suggests there is a liquid ocean. Europa could have all the essential ingredients needed for life: water, chemistry and energy (radiation blasted onto the moon from Jupiter may create fuel for life in the ocean below its surface).

Beyond Europa, orbiting around the planet Saturn are two more moons which may harbour life – Enceladus (another world with a frozen surface and a probable liquid ocean) and Titan (the only moon in our solar system with an atmosphere, which can be best thought of as similar to a young Earth). Even the planet Venus, a place once deemed inhospitable, may harbour simple life adrift in its clouds. Through studying the places where life survives on Earth, we've learned that it can exist in more extreme environments than we first thought. Some four kilometres under the ocean in the depths of the Mariana Trench lives the Dumbo octopus. There are at least 15 different kinds of these octopus-type creature, resembling what we might imagine an alien to look like. They were named 'Dumbo' after the Disney character on account of their ear-like fins. These small creatures exist in the dark, at a pressure that would crush a human.

Further into the remote depths of the ocean, we are discovering yet more life in conditions so extreme we did not think it could be there, but it is. Knowing the alien-like life that we are finding in the depths of our own ocean, and knowing there are probable liquid oceans elsewhere in the solar system, is helping us to understand the potential for life to exist in seemingly unhabitable places beyond Earth.

At the same time, we know that ours is not the only solar system. It is likely that trillions and trillions of other worlds exist beyond our own. And that's not even including all the moons orbiting these far-off worlds. The number of confirmed exoplanets – planets that orbit other stars – is currently in the thousands, and we are learning that it is likely there are more planets than stars in our universe.

Perhaps the biggest question is not just 'is there life?', but 'is there intelligent life?'. The Drake equation tries to quantify what the chances are of intelligent life existing elsewhere in our universe. Devised in the 1960s, it takes into account factors such as the rate of star formation in our universe, the number of stars with planetary systems and the fraction of planets in which life actually appears. Of course, the numerical inputs into this equation are just estimates at best, but even with the lowest numbers the chances are we have some cosmic neighbours.

Maybe there are civilisations out there that are so advanced that they know of us but they just pass us by, in much the same way that you wouldn't stop to have a conversation with ants that you passed in the street. Or perhaps there are civilisations like our own that have not yet developed the capabilities of travelling far from home. Maybe we are all anchored to our shores, unable to reach each other over the horizon. When you look up at the stars in the sky, it is possible that someone or something elsewhere in our universe is looking up and looking back at you. Our universe is not only as strange as you can imagine – it is *stranger* than you can imagine.

Of course, we still don't know how life comes to be – so our own existence and that of all other life on Earth could be an extremely rare event. To quote the cosmologist Carl Sagan, 'Extraordinary claims require extraordinary evidence' – and we do not yet have that extraordinary evidence. But we are getting there. Indeed, some of the scientists who work at the forefront of this field say it is a case of *when* not *if* we are able to prove we are not the only life in the universe. Even if it is just simple life elsewhere in our solar system, it is a discovery whose impact we perhaps cannot fully comprehend.

Our space age is in its infancy. Even with our advances in science, we know so little about what we are a part of. It is only through the new technology we are developing that, step by step, we will be able to edge out beyond our Earthly home and explore and uncover the mysteries that await us. It may take many human lifetimes to push out further into our solar system, and we will undoubtedly face unforeseen hurdles along the way, but our endeavours to meet great technological challenges will not cease. The entrepreneurs, mavericks, scientists, engineers and adventurers who are, in their own fields and in their own ways, right now working on the next thing that will help us push further into space, for longer, are not that different to the Magellans, the Captain Cooks or the von Brauns of our past. Who knows what sort of spacecraft will soon be taking its place alongside the *Wright Flyer*, the *Spirit of St Louis* and SpaceShipOne in the Smithsonian Museum, symbolising our continuing story of invention and discovery.

Maybe we were born too early to see many of the great wonders that are out there, but we are laying the foundations for our species to go further and build on both our successes and our failures. The possibilities to come from space – all of the worlds yet to be discovered and the human-made 'stars' in the night sky – fill me with hope. And all of us are living in a time when we are making those first permanent steps into our universe possible.

Chapter Five

LOOK BACK

'We came all this way to explore the Moon, and the most important thing is that we discovered the Earth.'

Bill Anders

I t is only from the vantage point of space that we are truly able to understand our Earth – a perspective that has been made possible by leaving our planet. Humans have always looked up at the night sky and wondered what was above us. Then, in the twentieth century, we figured out how to get to space, and we did something we had never done before: we looked back. When we finally made that journey 'up', the most powerful effects came not from pushing the limits of exploration but from seeing our own planet from afar.

Every single person who has travelled to space has been able to peer out of their spacecraft window and look back at our planet. For the rest of us, we are now able to take for granted the many photographs which exist of our Earth, taken by both people and robotic spacecraft. Before the Space Age, no one had ever seen the powerful image of our planet hanging in the darkness of space; most importantly, it gave us a new sense of our smallness and fragility, and highlighted our insignificance within the cosmos.

The number of people who have left the Earth is low – still a matter of hundreds. But what will happen as more people are able to go into space? If you could leave our planet and spend some time looking back at Earth against the inhospitable, infinite void of space; if you could see swirling white clouds, deep blue oceans, the arid deserts and night-time cities lit up by many millions of invisible people, do you think you would come back the same person? How might this amazing experience change you? And how would it change us, as a species, and our attitude to our planet, if many more of us could go and take a look for ourselves?

If you could visit the International Space Station, around 250 miles above our heads, you would be able to see the Earth's continents and great oceans pass by underneath you in a mere 90 minutes. Places that were once the frontier of our species, which seemed so large and foreboding to explorers like Ferdinand Magellan 500 years ago, go by in less time than it takes to watch a movie. Even from a distance of little more than a couple of hundred miles 'up', you have no sense of the borders that divide us and you begin to understand that our planet is really quite small.

If you were to travel further away, to the Moon – a place that only a small number of human beings have visited – our planet is far enough away that it would look like a large version of the Moon in our sky on Earth. Now our world is a blue marble, with swirling clouds set against the darkness of space. It's beautiful, but you can't see any sign of human life from here. Our Earth now looks simply like a planet, not a home.

But though it is on average 238,855 miles away, in terms of the solar system our closest celestial neighbour is still essentially on our front porch. By way of comparison, your average long-haul commercial airline pilot will clock up around 400,000 miles a year.

From the Moon's orbit you would be able to look back, just like the crew of Apollo 8 and subsequent lunar missions did, and see the entire Earth through your spacecraft window.

Our planet, which seems so grand and important, can be seen from a new perspective; from this distance, 'it' and 'we', with just our moon as a companion, are surrounded by the vastness of space and appear a long way from anything else.

While the Moon is the furthest people have travelled into space, robotic explorers have of course ventured further, beaming back pictures from deeper within our solar system. Viewed from the planet Mars, Earth is the brightest object at twilight, but not much bigger than a star in the night sky. From the Martian surface, it is only by using powerful cameras to look back that you can make out details of Earth, such as the continents, the oceans and swirls of clouds. It's now clear that the greatest achievement in human exploration – travelling to the Moon and returning safely to Earth – is but a small step when seen against the scale of our inner solar system.

Further back, to the planet Saturn. It was here, on 19 July 2013, that NASA's Cassini space probe sent back a picture of the Earth nestled beneath the rings of Saturn, the gas giant and second-largest planet in our solar system. Taken from almost 900 million miles away, Earth is now a small, pale blue dot. This date is also known as 'the day the Earth smiled' – named after a series of worldwide events to celebrate life on planet Earth and human accomplishments in exploring our solar system, on the day the photo was taken.

Today, in the twenty-first century, we are spoiled by photographs of our planet, and yet we know they do not compare with the impact of seeing it with your own eyes. 'It is the thing I remember most, the Earth from a great distance,' explained Michael Collins, of his experience on Apollo 11. 'Tiny, blue and white, bright, beautiful, serene and fragile. You don't get the full flavour looking at it [in photographs]. It doesn't sparkle like a little gem.'

Almost every astronaut who has been to space talks of being unprepared for what they see out of their spacecraft window or – even more powerful – the experience of a spacewalk. The human eye can pick up so much more than any photograph can show us. Many speak of the intense blackness of space contrasting against the fragile shell of our biosphere, and the realisation that it is protecting everything that is dear to them. The late Space Shuttle astronaut Willie McCool described this view as being beyond the imagination 'until you get up and see it and experience it and feel it'.

While photographs taken of the Earth from space are profound and have helped to shape modern thinking, for those few who have made the journey 'up', the complexity and fragility of our home planet goes from being something that they *know* to something that is *experienced*. Imagine being able to watch storms dance across our planet, to experience the aurora from space, with milky hues of green, blue and pink flickering across Earth. Imagine seeing that fragile blue line that represents all that is keeping us alive with your own eyes.

This view of our Earth was enough to move the astronaut Alan Shepard to tears as he stood on the surface of the Moon in 1971. Alan Shepard was a hardened naval aviator, an alpha male and an all-American hero who had, only a decade earlier, become the first American to ever travel to space. He was not the sort of person you would associate with being emotional. And yet he told his biographer that, standing on the Moon and looking up at our Earth from this distance in the vastness of space, he had started to cry, as our planet seemed so 'finite' and 'fragile'.

When we first went into space at the height of the Cold War, it was part of a race for technological supremacy over a hostile power, so unsurprisingly no one really considered the psychological effects of seeing Earth from space might have on astronauts. Scientists at NASA and the Soviet space programme thought a lot about the physical impact of going into space; the first astronauts went through intense medical testing, and crews for the first three lunar landings even spent 21 days in quarantine after returning from the Moon, in case they may have brought back deadly pathogens (although the Moon turned out to be barren and devoid of all life). But something incredible happened to many of those first space explorers. We sent tough, trained military personnel, logical people with backgrounds in science and engineering, and found that when they came back their whole outlook on life changed.

When Jim Irwin became the eighth of the twelve humans to walk on the Moon, it moved him to devote the rest of his life to his faith, despite not being a particularly committed Christian before he set off on Apollo 15. In 1972, the year after he returned from the Moon, Jim Irwin quit his job at NASA and founded his own religious organisation. He explained his lunar religious epiphany in these words: 'That beautiful, warm living object looked so fragile, so delicate, that if you touched it with a finger it would crumble and fall apart. Seeing this has to change a man, has to make a man appreciate the creation of God and the love of God.'

Bill Anders, who took the iconic *Earthrise* photo during the Apollo 8 mission, found that the view of the Earth from space changed his religious beliefs too, though not in the same way. Some years later he would say, 'The idea that things rotate around the Pope and up there is a big supercomputer wondering whether Billy was a good boy yesterday? It doesn't make sense.' And yet this view of our Earth still gave him a new perspective on just how fragile our planet is, where national borders seemed irrelevant.

Alan 'Al' Bean, the fourth human to walk on the Moon as part of the crew of Apollo 12, was inspired to turn to art. In 1981, he left NASA, but rather than go into politics, or take up a lucrative corporate position as many former astronauts have done, he became a full-time artist. For Alan, painting was the best way to share his experiences and express what he saw and felt as he walked on the Moon. He is no longer with us, but his paintings remain – the first ever to be created by someone who visited another world.

This psychological effect that the first-hand experience of seeing the Earth from space has on that person has a name; it is known as the 'overview effect'. The term was coined in the 1980s, after more and more astronauts started describing the effect that seeing the Earth from space had on them. It was invented not by a space traveller, but by a writer, philosopher and Harvard graduate by the name of Frank White. (Which in many ways is an excellent example of why, while science and technology push us forward in our endeavours, we need creative minds to attempt to comprehend and interpret what we are experiencing.)

The overview effect attempts to describe what is known as 'the cognitive shift in awareness' that comes from seeing our planet from space. The concept of space and our true smallness in the universe is pretty incomprehensible to almost all of us here on Earth. We know we exist on a planet, and that there are other planets out there. Our Earth is huge to us, on our human scale, yet we are simultaneously aware that in the vastness of space it is but a speck – even though the concept remains so mind-bogglingly unrelatable to much of our everyday life. But if you can actually go into space and see our Earth from afar, that makes it real. It turns the knowledge that we are a planet floating in an unimaginably large cosmos into an all-encompassing experience.

How could the experience not change you? It's a new perspective on our home, but it's one that in many ways is … unnatural. We have evolved to survive and thrive on Earth, but our ingenuity has allowed us to fashion the tools to enable us to leave our planet and reach space – a place where biologically we are not meant to be.

People who have experienced it sometimes describe the overview effect as being overcome by emotion, or coming to see themselves differently, or feeling a renewed sense of purpose or change in attitude after returning to Earth. From space you not only realise how beautiful our planet is and how small it is, but also how delicate it is. Astronauts often return with a newfound respect for our home and with concern for the damage we are doing to it. Others realise that, while our planet is beautiful, it is unfair; they discover an overwhelming desire to do good for others and address the huge inequality that exists on Earth.

It is both powerful and humbling to realise that, on this grander scale, many of the materialistic things we hold so dear, and the arguments and conflicts which seem so important, matter less than we tend to think. These views can give us a new awareness of who we are, and a new appreciation for what we have. This is true on a personal, national and planetary scale.

It's a well-worn cliché that, from space, countries have no borders. Space travellers who look back at our planet don't see individual states or nations, they only see the shapes of continents and oceans. The view from space doesn't show divisions. Seeing the Earth like this helps us to understand that we are all in this together.

*

The words 'climate emergency' have now begun to appear in the headlines with a frightening regularity. There is frustration in many quarters that our politicians and business leaders are not doing enough to protect our fragile planet from the damage caused by its human population.

But what would happen if we could send politicians or policy makers into space? Those responsible for making decisions that affect our planet's future? It is a notion that has long been mused upon by astronauts. For those who look back at Earth do not just experience the beauty of our home; from the International Space Station it's possible to quite clearly see damage being inflicted on our planet, from the shrinking of the Aral Sea to the polluted air over industrial zones and the burning of the Amazon rainforest.

At the end of 2015, at the United Nations Climate Change Conference in Paris, world leaders reached an agreement to combat climate change, which would later become known as the Paris Agreement. While it was an important global agreement which served to acknowledge what is happening to our planet, for many the recommended actions did not go far enough.

Ahead of discussions, attendees were played a video message titled 'Call to Earth', featuring a group of astronauts speaking of their experiences looking back at Earth. Among the astronauts in the video was Nicole Stott, who expressed her wish that the meeting could be held from the ISS, not only because of 'the beautiful horizon-to-horizon view of our planet as your backdrop' but because 'there would be nothing better for reinforcing the significance of what you are doing'.

Just imagine for a moment what the impact on that meeting could have been if those making the decisions were to not only see the data given to them by scientists, but to experience it in this way. If the world leaders could have looked out of the window of the ISS for themselves and seen that thin blue line which protects us from the inhospitable void of space, what might the overview effect have done for the agreements made in Paris that December?

We know that the recognition of the fragility of our planet has reduced the most hardened military personnel to tears and profoundly changed the outlook of those who have been able to leave it and look back. So perhaps it is not naïve to think that if those who wield power were able to take stock in this way, even just for a few moments, then the experience could shift their thinking. Surely it would be hard to hide behind the idea that maybe 'scientists have got it wrong', or that economic considerations are the most important considerations, when you can see for yourself not only the effects of climate change, but just how precious our home really is. Perhaps the experience of seeing the Earth from space has the potential to save us …

While he was on the ISS, Canadian astronaut Chris Hadfield tweeted: 'Karachi, Pakistan. More than 20 million of us live in this thriving delta city.' In a subsequent interview, he said that the significance of the word 'us' had only occurred to him later. Chris isn't from Pakistan, but from his viewpoint 250 miles 'up' he wasn't really thinking about nationalities anymore, just human beings as residents of Earth.

And when astronauts return to Earth from space, they often don't land in their home country, yet when they step off back onto land, the ground crew and television commentary still welcome them 'home'. When American NASA astronauts flew on the Soyuz, though they would land in Kazakhstan on the other side of the world, they were still home. From space, Earth is our home.

On a cosmic scale, we are not divided; we are united as citizens of planet Earth. It is one thing to simply talk about it, quite another to take in this all-encompassing and life-changing experience for yourself. Going into space and looking back at Earth changes the way we look at ourselves.

In many ways our Earth can be thought of as being like a spaceship, and all of us, plus all of the other species with which we share this world, as crewmates. We are all in this together. And just like any other crew on a ship, we hold the responsibility to look after the vessel carrying us. Photographs like *Earthrise,* and the iconic *Blue Marble* view of the whole Earth taken by the crew of Apollo 17, helped to show that although we may think we are divided – by nation, country or continent – in space we are united as inhabitants of one unlikely planet.

*

Often those who have been to space care about our planet with a newfound depth of feeling and love, which it's hard to fully appreciate unless you have experienced it for yourself. Among them is a man called Piers Sellers, someone you have probably never heard of, but who dedicated his life to protecting Earth, a calling that was amplified through his experiences in space.

Piers was born in England but became an American citizen to fulfil his dreams of space. As a NASA astronaut, he spacewalked six times and helped to build the International Space Station. He received an OBE in 2011 (a nomination that was endorsed by none other than Neil Armstrong) and, on his final space mission, he flew bark from Sir Isaac Newton's famous apple tree into space. But Piers' main work and passion was being a climate scientist, a field to which he dedicated his life, trying to better understand how the Earth system works.

As an astronaut, Piers was fortunate enough to see how

'unbelievably beautiful' our planet is from space. But as one of the many climate scientists working at NASA, he contributed to our knowledge and understanding that we, as humans, are changing our planet, our home, in a potentially disastrous way.

While spacewalking, as the space station from which he had departed 'gleamed in the sunlight', he was able to watch as day on Earth turned into night and the Atlantic passed by below him. Rolling over the horizon, he started to see Europe, and the lights of the major cities below come on – cities full of millions of people, but from his position he was able to cover each with his hand. Later, Piers explained that this sight gave him a moment of inspiration: 'I've always had faith in humanity, but to see humanity living and breathing down there, somehow made me feel better.'

Looking back at Earth, he realised: 'All the creativity, arts, philosophy, science and engineering, everything that humans had achieved really came from these great cities.' He thought about how humans had evolved and come together to create the world we live in today, and decided that while human creativity had got us into the situation we currently face because of the damage done to our planet's climate system, it could also get us out of it.

This reinforced Piers' belief in the importance of addressing the threats to our fragile planet, but it also gave him a sense of optimism that we could work together towards the common goal of, as he put it, 'A planet that can continue to support life, including all of us.'

In January 2016, Piers wrote a piece for the *New York Times* entitled 'Cancer and Climate Change'. In it he mentioned that his personal horizon had been 'steeply foreshortened'; Piers was terminally ill with stage four pancreatic cancer – he would not live to see the end of that year. Yet instead of lamenting his situation, he used the piece as an opportunity to tell the world why we must continue to study, understand and develop technology to combat climate change. He explained how, following his diagnosis, he had drawn up a 'bucket list' before realising that he did not want to spend his remaining time on Earth 'jostling with tourists on a beach'. Instead, the most important thing for him was to continue his work at NASA, managing scientists as they study the Earth system.

In his final year of life, he continued to work towards a better understanding of changes in the Earth's atmosphere, water and landmasses. He worked tirelessly, appearing in documentaries, television shows and doing interviews for journalists, all while terminally ill. He used his remaining time on Earth to continue his work on a problem we all face. He did so not because he was pessimistic, but because he had hope. As Piers wrote: 'I am optimistic for our future. And so I am going to work tomorrow.' So must we all.

Piers died in December 2016 at the age of 61. While he might no longer be with us, his words of optimism and passion for our planet live on through those that he worked with and inspired. I interviewed Piers when I was a young weather presenter working for the BBC in 2010, and his passion for space and science and his optimism for the future filled me with hope and reminded me of my own dreams of space. He was both charismatic and inspiring, and my meeting with him would help set me on my path to working in the space industry full-time. After reading the *New York Times* piece some years later, I decided to nominate him for the Space Foundation's General James E. Hill Lifetime Space Achievement Award – a prestigious award in the US, previous winners of which have included Neil Armstrong and Buzz Aldrin. Piers won, and the award was presented posthumously in the spring of 2017, at a bittersweet event in Colorado.

I closed my nomination letter by stating that 'the world needs more people like Piers'. For all of the problems we face in the world, there are so many scientists working to create a better future for us all. I believe that space has the capacity to bring out the best in us. And the combination of both scientists and the valuable information we can gather from leaving Earth can offer us the opportunity to look after our planet and persuade those in power to make changes. Just as Piers was able to do. Hopefully, reading this, you too feel inspired that, at a time when there are so many reasons to be pessimistic for our future, there are clever, optimistic people working to create a better tomorrow for us all.

*

So far, though, nearly everyone who has been to space has been a scientist, an engineer, military personnel or a combination of all three. We have been sending the same type of people into space – physically strong, technically minded – because the rigours and complexities of space travel have required those skillsets. But of course, they represent just a small fraction of who we are as a species.

The reality is that the overwhelming majority of people who have so far travelled to space have been white and male. Our first ambassadors into this new frontier do not represent the diversity of who we are on Earth. But if we are to move forward successfully as a species into space, then the type of people we send is going to need to change.

Private companies such as Virgin Galactic and Blue Origin are working on transforming going into space from being a profession to being an experience, accessible to many more people. Just as with flight in the early part of the twentieth century, there's no doubt that those initial passengers will largely be drawn from the wealthiest and most privileged. In the immediate future, it will continue to cost huge amounts of money to take a short trip to space on a sub-orbital flight to experience weightlessness and a view of our Earth for essentially just a matter of minutes.

However, just as in the early days of air travel, technology will evolve and prices will most likely come down, giving more people the opportunity to experience seeing our planet in this new way. In fact, this is something we are already starting to see happen.

The first ever space tourist was Dennis Tito, an American

businessman who, in 2001, travelled to space as a passenger alongside professional astronauts. He paid a reported $20 million for his ticket to launch on the Russian Soyuz and enjoy a six-day stay on the ISS. Today, prices for sub-orbital trips sit around the half-million-dollar mark. This is an extraordinary sum, beyond the reach of most of us here on Earth, but it does represent a significant price drop nonetheless.

Will these wealthy few who go first on these new types of tourist trips to space come back changed, as many of the space explorers who came before them did? Of those who talk about wanting to go into space, the experience of looking back at planet Earth is one of the most common reasons given.

While there's no getting away from the fact that the first generation of space tourists are going to be primarily drawn from the ranks of the exceedingly wealthy, there is still a shift towards a different type of person going into space. The new space tourists are artists, writers, business people, musicians – some even represent countries where no citizen has yet been to space. Canadian businessman Guy Laliberté – who came from a performing arts background and went on to found Cirque du Soleil – dedicated his spaceflight to raising awareness of access to safe water for the world's poorest. And American-Iranian Anousheh Ansari was the first person to be born in Iran to go to space (and the first female space tourist) in 2006.

How will the first generations of space tourists be able to communicate what they experience in a way that those who have gone before them have not? Unlike professional astronauts, space tourists – or 'spaceflight participants', as they are also known – don't have to be focused on the technicalities of the mission. Instead they are able to 'sit back, relax and enjoy the flight', as their whole reason for going to space is for the experience and to see our Earth in a new way. They will have different communities, different audiences and, in some cases, different 'fans' to the traditional astronauts who have been before them.

Imagine, for example, what would happen if a famous singer took a trip into space. While there has been music recorded in orbit – the Canadian astronaut Chris Hadfield even released an album recorded on the ISS – no one who is a musician first and foremost has experienced space. How would the impact of seeing the Earth in this way change them? And how would they tell their story, of this experience of seeing our planet and just how fragile and lonely it is, to millions of fans who may never have thought much about space before, through their music? With the birth of space tourism come new ways of telling the story not only of space, but of Earth.

Do you personally know anyone who has been to space? Statistically it's highly unlikely that you do. But would you feel differently about space if you knew someone who had left our planet? Would it feel more 'real' and less like an impossible dream? As the number of space tourists increases, so will the number of people who have a link to someone who has had this experience. This takes space travel from being something unrelatable and makes it something that more people feel connected to.

While in many ways NASA – with its visitor centres, live launch coverage and social media channels with millions of followers – still leads the way in communicating the story of space to us, just think for a moment about all the new people who could be inspired if, for example, a 19-year-old 'influencer' were posting from space. Or an 80-year-old grandmother were able to go. Who might their story reach? The more of our kind who are able to truly realise that we are all in this together, the more we will be able to enact change here on Earth.

One of my favourite places that I visited to talk about space is Uganda. In rural parts of the country, far from light pollution, with its tropical climate and pleasant night-time temperatures, you can look out at the stars with a sense of wonder that is absent in large cities full of bright lights. Despite many living in poverty, people in these remote areas know a lot about space, often having grown up living beneath the stars, their evenings lit by the glow of our moon.

Not only is there an appreciation for the wonder of our universe, but also the desire to go there. It was in Uganda that I met Robert, a 30-year-old airport taxi driver. He grew up in a remote village with no electricity, yet he is fascinated by space. He spends much of his time waiting at the airport but has never taken a flight, and to him going to space would be a 'dream come true'. Uganda is far from having its own space programme, but Robert believes seeing the Earth from above would change his life, as well as enable him to inspire others from his home country when he told them about what he saw.

It is easy for us in the West to assume that those in developing countries don't have an interest in space and the benefits to come from it, but they do. Imagine if Robert were able to go to space – how might those in his own community relate to him in a way they probably couldn't to a white, Western astronaut? How many lives could he touch by sharing his experiences? The more people who make the journey 'up' from different and diverse communities, the more people will be inspired by the stories of someone they can relate to.

Over the course of this book, I've made comparisons between the early days of aviation and where we are now with human spaceflight. However, when we talk about the need to make space truly about all of us on this planet, this is where the comparison between flight and our space future stops. While many of us take getting on a plane for work or holidays for granted, roughly 80 per cent of the world's population have never taken a flight.

As you read this, people are striving to increase the number of people who will have the opportunity to see Earth from space. Even though the price tag is still large, it doesn't necessarily mean those funding the trips will be the ones travelling. There are initiatives aimed at sending people from all kinds of backgrounds to space, with the trips paid for by a combination of donations by wealthy individuals and corporate sponsorship. What they are effectively doing is democratising access to space, granting to those who go the gift of perspective. After all, if we want to take those first steps towards being a multi-planetary, not just a one-planet, species, space needs to be about all of us. We need to all be on board. There is no point striving forward into space if it is just going to further divide us. To succeed in space, we need to involve and inspire as many people as we can – after all, who knows where the next big, creative, game-changing idea will come from.

Democratising access to space is about making it feel like something that is both relevant and accessible to us all, not just something 'out there' studied by scientists, where 'normal people' have zero chance of ever going. Inspiration matters. Looking up and wondering about what lies beyond us is something that connects us all globally. If we are to successfully move forward into space, we must all be in this together.

*

Imagine one day getting into a spacecraft and going to space yourself. Perhaps it still feels like an impossible dream? But we only need to reflect on our own history to see how far we have come. Think of what someone born in the year 1900 would have seen in the course of their lifetime – the birth of flight, humans travelling to space, humans on the Moon. The advent of the television and computing.

Numerous medical advances which transformed human life expectancy. If you are in your mid-thirties or older, you probably remember the first time you went on the internet. If you are in your late sixties or older, you might remember the first family on your street to get a television. Things that once seemed beyond the realms of possibility are now things that we take for granted. The acceleration of technology is exponential and we cannot even begin to imagine what is to come.

Soon we will witness the next humans to set foot on the Moon and see images of our Earth taken from its surface – no longer photographs from history or ones taken by robotic explorers, but photographs taken by people on the lunar surface at that exact moment, and broadcast to you in real time. We will be able to go outside and look up at the Moon, and know that there are people there looking back at us.

Michael Collins had a unique way of thinking about both who we are and where we are going in space. On Apollo 11's voyage to the Moon, the spacecraft was bathed in constant sunlight on its voyage and had to be slowly rotated in order to control the temperature – something Michael likened to a 'a chicken on a barbeque spit'. As they turned, the Earth and then the Moon would appear in their window. The crew could choose between looking towards the Moon, which represented the future, and where Neil Armstrong and Buzz Aldrin would soon be landing to make history, or they could look back towards

Earth, our home and where they had come from. The crew looked both ways. And that is what we must do.

No matter where we go or what we do in space, Earth will always be our home. It is both fragile and beautiful. It is a place full of problems caused by many centuries of human life – and this feels never more relevant than now. But by going to space and looking back, we have the opportunity to address our problems in a new way.

Many problems existed on Earth in 1969, too, but the Apollo 11 mission went ahead. The lunar landing not only united so many across the planet who watched it – and who would always remember where they were when it happened – but also generations to come. The first mission to see a human being set foot on another world forever changed who we are as a species. Many centuries from now, when you and I are long gone, history will still recall the first moment humans left Earth and set foot on another world.

If our ancestors had stopped exploring Earth while problems still raged, we would not have the world we live in today. For as we have explored and pushed forward, this has enabled technology and new knowledge, which has benefited all. Now we have the ability to go to space, we need to use it to improve life on Earth, but we also must not stop moving forward. As Michael Collins put it to Congress in the autumn of 1969, not long after he returned from his lunar mission, 'Man has always gone where he has been able to go. It is that simple.'

That desire to know what is over that 'next hill' is what

makes us human. I would argue that stasis is not good for us and if we don't move forward to not only explore but to utilise space, we are essentially remaining still. We cannot do that. Just as we can explore far beyond where our ancestors did, our curiosity today will give way to a new freedom to explore for our descendants far beyond what we can imagine, just like our freedoms now are beyond what those who came before us could imagine. We owe it to future generations to keep moving forward.

Yet for all our ambitions and dreams of space, we still don't really know what is 'out there'; we are only just beginning to scratch the surface. Even when humans travel beyond the Moon, beyond Mars, beyond Pluto and to the edge of our solar system, we will still only just be beginning our voyages in space. We are so impossibly tiny in the vastness of this universe and so many wonders await us. And for all the answers we gain about this weird and wonderful cosmos that we are a part of, we are just left with more questions. It is both exciting and terrifying to think about.

For me, it is the ability to see ourselves and our home for what we really are, against the backdrop of the universe, that gives me the greatest hope for humanity. Just like how stopping and looking up at the stars – even for just a second – can be both humbling and terrifying, the ability for more and more people to be able to look back at our world will change us. When I think about how much looking up has influenced my own life, I can only begin to imagine how the ability for more of us to look back (myself included) could change our attitudes and appreciation towards Earth.

Seeing our planet from space has the potential to help us rethink the way we address issues on Earth. Both in a practical sense, as we can use data from satellites to monitor changes to our planet, and in a more philosophical sense, as it gives us the perspective to think more about who we are. One of the things that this view has shown us is that we are a long way from anything else; nobody is coming to help us. We are responsible for ourselves and for looking after our home. If anything happens, on a cosmic scale we would not be missed. The Earth may be significant to us, but to the universe it is not.

Earth will always be our home. We are at the perfect distance from our sun for life as we know it to exist. For the conditions to be just right for our planet to be what it is. To sustain the life that it does. To sustain us. Of all of the worlds we know about and will probably go on to discover, none will be quite like this beautiful blue marble. It is our oasis in the unforgiving void of space. It is irreplaceable. It is our first spaceship and we must look after it.

We go into space not to escape, but for the good of our species. We simply do not know what is out there or what is to come. And even though the questions we have will not be answered in mere lifetimes, we are still all part of this adventure. In pushing the boundaries of what we can achieve, in remaining forever curious, we all touch the future. There is no greater story.

Keep looking up and know that, one day, future generations of our kind will be looking back at our Earth from deep within the vastness of our solar system, remembering all of us who were driven by that urge to explore.

I am optimistic for our future, wherever we may go.

To the stars.

To be continued...

ACKNOWLEDGEMENTS

T his book is for the dreamers. The ones who have gone before us and the ones who will continue to go against the status quo. The ones who make the impossible possible and dream of a life that we cannot yet imagine. We owe our future to them.

All great endeavours require a great team, and I could not have completed this book without so many amazing people supporting me in various ways. So thank you to everyone who has done so.

In particular, I wanted to write some words for three very special ladies who have helped me immensely. To my literary agent Lauren Gardner, thank you for turning the news on back in 2017 to see me talking enthusiastically about space. This book has been a long time in the making, and I am so grateful for how hard you worked to find the perfect publisher. All those long meetings and hours spent rehashing draft proposals were worth it.

To Kate Fox at HQ, thank you for believing in me and my passion, and letting me write the book I wanted to write. I am so grateful for the opportunity you gave me.

And to my editor Liz Marvin, thank you for getting me through to the end of this book. Your support has been incredible, you have been there for me seven days a week and you have pushed me to do my best.

And finally, to the fallen heroes – all those who gave their lives to help pave the way for our space future. They live forever in all that we will achieve.

INDEX

B

C

from space 8–9, 24, 27, 77, 86, 148–9, 162–9, 173, 176, 219–46
unity of humans 20, 24–5, 56, 57, 89, 229–30

E

Earthrise 166, 167, 224, 230
eclipses, ancient view 37
Edison, Thomas 187
Einstein, Albert 44
Enceladus 211
Endeavour 41–2, 47
escape velocity 190–1
Esnault-Pelterie, Robert 46–7
Europa 26, 210
Explorer 1 60
extra-terrestrial life 19, 29
    intelligent 212–13
    in our solar system 19, 142, 210–11, 213

F

Falcon 9 rocket 182, 193
Falcon Heavy rocket 181–2
financial transactions 150–1
Fireball XL5 140
firefighters' equipment 145–6
'First Moon Flights' Club 139–40, 144
food, and spaceflight 198–9
Freeman, Theodore 110
frozen water, mining in space 199–200

G

Gagarin, Yuri 60–1, 70, 84, 110, 141
galaxies 18, 20, 97
Gemini program 67–9, 71, 102, 121
    Gemini 6 67, 69
    Gemini 7 67, 69
    Gemini 8 71
General James E Hill Lifetime Space Achievement Award 233

J

K

L